Raspberry Pi

Weight Sensing, Emergency Light, Color Sensor TCS3200, Android App over Bluetooth, PyGame Library etc,..

ANBAZHAGAN K

Raspberry Pi - Weight Sensing, Emergency Light, Color Sensor TCS3200, Android App over Bluetooth, PyGame Library etc,..

CONTENTS

with Raspberry Pi

ACKNOWLEDGMENTS

The writer might want to recognize the diligent work of the article group in assembling this book. He might likewise want to recognize the diligent work of the Raspberry Pi Foundation and the Arduino bunch for assembling items and networks that help to make the Internet of Things increasingly open to the overall population. Yahoo for the democratization of innovation!

INTRODUCTION

The Internet of Things (IOT) is a perplexing idea comprised of numerous PCs and numerous correspondence ways. Some IOT gadgets are associated with the Internet and some are most certainly not. Some IOT gadgets structure swarms that convey among themselves. Some are intended for a solitary reason, while some are increasingly universally useful PCs. This book is intended to demonstrate to you the IOT from the back to front. By structure IOT gadgets, the per user will comprehend the essential ideas and will almost certainly develop utilizing the rudiments to make his or her very own IOT applications. These included ventures will tell the per user the best way to assemble their very own IOT ventures and to develop the models appeared. The significance of Computer Security in IOT gadgets is additionally talked about and different systems for protecting the IOT from unapproved clients or programmers. The most significant takeaway from this book is in structure the tasks yourself.

1. STEP BY STEP INSTRUCTIONS TO FIND IP ADDRESS OF RASPBERRY PI UTILIZING PYTHON SCRIPT

The principle issue while working with Raspberry Pi is to realize the IP address of the Raspberry Pi, which will be expected to login into it utilizing some SSH or record move customer. He will share some Python contents to locate the nearby IP address of your Raspberry Pi on the system and show it on the 16x2 LCD Screen. We will likewise include the content in the Crontab so it very well may be run on at regular intervals and we will have the refreshed IP address without fail.

Interfacing 16x2 LCD with Raspberry Pi:

Before we will discover the IP address of the Raspberry PI, initially we have to interface 16x2 Liquid Crystal Display with Raspberry Pi. Here we have utilized an outside Adafruit Library for interfacing the 16x2 LCD with Raspberry Pi, utilizing which you don't have to compose numerous lines of code to drive the LCD and you can legitimately print on LCD by simply utilizing one line of code. Anyway this Library is made by Adafruit however it can utilized for any Liquid Crystal Display module that has HD44780 controller.

To utilize the Adafruit Library, we first need to introduce it by utilizing underneath directions. First order will clone the CharLCD archive (by Adafruit) on your Raspberry Pi, 2nd direction will take you within the installed registry lastly we have to execute setup.py content, exhibited inside the Adafruit_Python-_CharLCD index, to introduce the library.

```
git    clone    https://github.com/adafruit/Adafruit_Python_CharLCD.git

cd ./Adafruit_Python_CharLCD

sudo python setup.py install
```

Presently the library for 16x2 LCD has been introduced and you can utilize its capacities by simply bringing in this library in your python program utilizing the underneath line:

```
import Adafruit_CharLCD as LCD
```

There are some model contents inside the 'models' envelope which is available in the library organizer (Adafruit_Python_CharLCD). You can examine the arrangement by running char_lcd.py model content. However, before that, you have to associate the LCD pins with the Raspberry Pi as given underneath in the circuit chart in next area.

You can likewise associate LCD with some other GPIO pins of Raspberry Pi, all you have to specify the right interfacing pins in your python program like beneath. Become familiar with Raspberry Pi GPIO Pins here.

```
# Raspberry Pi pin setup

lcd_rs = 18

lcd_en = 23

lcd_d4 = 24

lcd_d5 = 16
```

```
lcd_d6 = 20

lcd_d7 = 21

lcd_backlight = 2
```

Presently you can straightforwardly utilize the capacities gave by Adafruit Library to control the LCD. A portion of the capacities are given underneath; you can discover more in model content:

- lcd.message(message) = To print the content on LCD.

- lcd.clear() = To clear the LCD.

- set_cursor(col, push) = Move the cursor to any situation at segment and column.

- lcd.blink(True) = To squint the cursor (True or False)

- lcd.move_left() = To shift the cursor to Left by one position.

- lcd.move_right() = To shift the cursor to Right by one position.

In case you need to interface the LCD without utilizing any outer library, at that point you can check our past instructional exercise, where we have composed every one of the capacities for 16x2 LCD. Check this one to interface the LCD in 8-piece Mode and this one to interface the LCD in 4-piece mode.

Circuit Diagram:

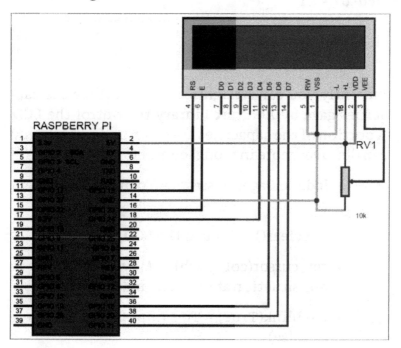

Display IP Address of Raspberry Pi on LCD:

In the wake of interfacing 16x2 LCD with Raspberry Pi, presently we have to get the IP address of Raspberry Pi and print it on LCD utilizing Python Script. There are part of approaches to get the nearby IP address of Raspberry Pi, here we are depicting three Python Scripts to get the IP address, you can utilize any of them.

Utilizing Linux Commands:

On terminal, we can without much of a stretch get the IP address by utilizing hostname - I direction, so in case we can run the linux order from the python, at that point we can get the IP address. So to run Linux directions from Python we have to import a library named directions, so the total program will resemble underneath:

```
import time

import Adafruit_CharLCD as LCD

import commands

# Raspberry Pi pin setup

lcd_rs = 18

lcd_en = 23

lcd_d4 = 24

lcd_d5 = 16

lcd_d6 = 20

lcd_d7 = 21

lcd_backlight = 2
```

```
# Define LCD column and row size for 16x2 LCD.

lcd_columns = 16

lcd_rows = 2

lcd   =   LCD.Adafruit_CharLCD(lcd_rs,   lcd_en,
lcd_d4,  lcd_d5,  lcd_d6,  lcd_d7,  lcd_columns,
lcd_rows, lcd_backlight)

lcd.message('Local IP Address:\n')

lcd.message(commands.getoutput('hostname -I'))

time.sleep(10.0) # Wait 5 seconds

lcd.clear()
```

You can likewise supplant the hostname - I order in the program by the beneath direction in case you need to get the IP address by utilizing progressively dependable ifconfig order:

lcd.message(commands.getoutput('ifconfig wlan0 | grep "inet\ addr" | cut - d: - f2 | cut - d" " - f1'))

Note: Repalce 'wlan0' with 'eth0' if your Raspberry Pi is on the Ethernet.

Utilizing Socket programming:

Here in this program we will make an attachment of family AF_INET and type SOCK_DGRAM utilizing this line: s = socket.socket(socket.AF_INET, socket. SOCK_DGRAM), at that point we will make association through the attachment utilizing some hostname or ip address like 8.8.8.8, you can use some other site to interface with the attachment like gmail.com. So we can get the neighborhood IP address of RPi from the attachment which has been made for correspondence between Raspberry Pi and sham IP address. The following is the full Program:

```
import time

import Adafruit_CharLCD as LCD

import socket

# Raspberry Pi pin setup

lcd_rs = 18

lcd_en = 23

lcd_d4 = 24

lcd_d5 = 16

lcd_d6 = 20
```

```
lcd_d7 = 21

lcd_backlight = 2

# Define LCD column and row size for 16x2 LCD.

lcd_columns = 16

lcd_rows = 2

lcd = LCD.Adafruit_CharLCD(lcd_rs, lcd_en,
lcd_d4, lcd_d5, lcd_d6, lcd_d7, lcd_columns,
lcd_rows, lcd_backlight)

def get_ip_address():

  ip_address = '';

  s = socket.socket(socket.AF_INET, socket.SOCK_D-
GRAM)

  s.connect((("8.8.8.8",80))

  ip_address = s.getsockname()[0]

  s.close()

  return ip_address

lcd.message('Local IP Address:\n')
```

```
lcd.message(get_ip_address())

# Wait 5 seconds

time.sleep(10.0)

lcd.clear()
```

Note:

Using "socket.gethostbyname(socket.gethost-name())" will consistently give you Localhost IP address (127.0.0.1)

Get familiar with Socket Programming in python here.

Utilizing 'fcntl' Module:

This module performs document control as well as Input/Output control on record descriptors. Here it is utilized to separate the IP address from the system documents. The following is the full Python code:

```
import time

import Adafruit_CharLCD as LCD

import socket
```

```
import fcntl

import struct

# Raspberry Pi pin setup

lcd_rs = 18

lcd_en = 23

lcd_d4 = 24

lcd_d5 = 16

lcd_d6 = 20

lcd_d7 = 21

lcd_backlight = 2

# Define LCD column and row size for 16x2 LCD.

lcd_columns = 16

lcd_rows = 2

lcd  =   LCD.Adafruit_CharLCD(lcd_rs,   lcd_en,
lcd_d4,  lcd_d5,  lcd_d6,  lcd_d7,  lcd_columns,
lcd_rows, lcd_backlight)
```

```
def get_interface_ipaddress(network):

    s = socket.socket(socket.AF_INET, socket.
SOCK_DGRAM)

  return socket.inet_ntoa(fcntl.ioctl(

    s.fileno(),

    0x8915, # SIOCGIFADDR

    struct.pack('256s', network[:15])

  )[20:24])

lcd.message('Local IP Address:\n')

lcd.message(get_interface_ipaddress('wlan0'))

# Wait 5 seconds

time.sleep(10.0)

lcd.clear()
```

Note:

Repalce 'wlan0' with 'eth0' if your Raspberry Pi is on the Ethernet.

Become familiar with utilizing 'fcnfl' Module here.

Execute Script Periodically using 'crontab':

Last advance is to include the passage for running this content intermittently on at regular intervals with the goal that we can get refreshed IP inevitably. To do this we have to alter the cron document utilizing underneath order:

```
crontab –e
```

And afterward enter the underneath line at the base of the cron record and spare it utilizing CTRL + X, at that point Y, at that point enter.

```
*/15 **** sudo python /home/pi/ip_address_lcd.py
```

You can change the location as indicated by area of your Python Script document and you can likewise change the term where you need over and over run the content to get the refreshed IP.

2. RASPBERRY PI BASED WEIGHT SENSING AUTOMATIC GATE

In this task we are going to utilize Load cell and HX711 Weight Sensor with Raspberry Pi to manufacture an Automatic Gate. We have seen these weight detecting entryways at numerous shopping centers and showrooms, which consequently opens when somebody is remaining close to the entryway and get shut after that individual is no more. Here we are additionally making a similar Automatic Gate which will detect the weight and get opened naturally and will stay open until that weight or weight will be there. This door will be shut naturally when the weight is expelled. This programmed door can likewise be constructed utilizing PIR sensor like here.

Here for showing reason, we have utilized basic DC engine as the entryway and a hard cardboard as a stage for putting the weight. In last instructional exercise, we have Interfaced Load Cell and HX711 with Arduino to gauge the loads. For more Raspberry Projects, check here.

Required Components:

- Raspberry Pi (any model should work)
- Load cell
- HX711 Load cell Amplifier Module
- DC motor otherwise Electric gate otherwise DVD trolley
- L293D Motor Driver IC
- Power source otherwise power bank

- 16x2 LCD
- Breadboard
- Connecting wires
- Nut bolts, Frame as well as base

Load Cell and HX711 Weight Sensor Module:

Burden cell is transducer which changes power or weight into electrical yield. Extent of this electrical yield is straightforwardly extent to the power being applied. Burden cells have strain check, which misshapes when weight is applied on it. And afterward strain check creates electrical sign on misshapening as its powerful opposition changes on disfigurement. A heap cell ordinarily comprises of 4 strain measures in a Wheatstone connect design. Burden cell comes in different reaches like 5kg, 10kg, 100kg and that's just the beginning, here we have utilized Load cell, which can weight upto 40kg.

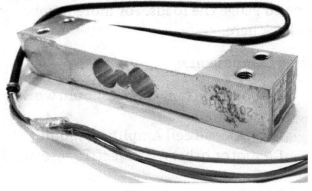

Presently the electrical sign created by Load cell is in hardly any millivolts, so they should be further enhance by some speaker and henceforth HX711 Weighing Sensor comes into picture. HX711 Weighing Sensor Module has HX711 chip, which is a 24 high accuracy A/D converter (Analog to computerized converter). HX711 has two simple information channels as well as we can get gain up to 128 by programming these channels. So HX711 module enhances the low electric yield of Load cells and afterward this intensified and carefully changed over sign is bolstered into the Arduino to infer the weight.

Burden cell is associated with HX711 Load cell Amplifier utilizing four wires. These four wires are Red, Black, White and Green/Blue. There might be slight variety in shades of wires from module to module. Beneath the association subtleties and chart:

- RED Wire is associated with E+

- Dark Wire is associated with E-

- WHITE Wire is associated with A-

- GREEN/BLUE Wire is associated with A+

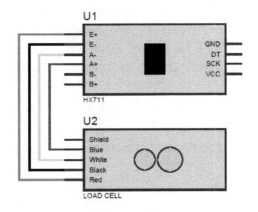

Fixing Load Cell with Platform and Base:

So as to make this entire arrangement work, we need to introduce Load Cell under the ground before the entryway, with the goal that it can detect the heaviness of individual remaining close to the entryway. Be that as it may, here for Demonstration reason, we have fixed the Load cell under a hard cardboard, which will fill in as a stage where we can put the weight and can test the door. Burden cell has additionally been fixed with Wooden Base with the assistance of stray pieces, so it will stay still. The following are a few photos of the arrangement:

Circuit Explanation:

Associations for this Automatic Gate venture are simple and schematic is given underneath. 16x2 LCD pins RS, EN, d4, d5, d6, and d7 are associated with GPIO pin number 18, 23, 24, 25, 8 and 7 of Raspberry Pi separately. HX711 Module's DT and SCK pins are legitimately associated with Raspberry Pi's GPIO pin 27 and 17 and Motor Driver L293D is associated at GPIO pin 12 and 16 of Raspberry Pi. Burden cell associations with HX711 module are as of now clarified before and furthermore appeared in the beneath circuit outline.

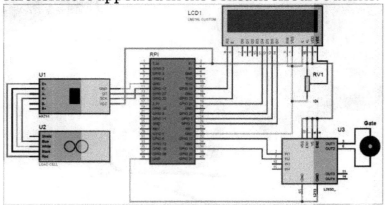

Working Explanation:

In this undertaking, we have utilized Raspberry Pi 3 to control entire the procedure. Burden cell detects the Pressure on the floor close to the entryway and supplies an electrical simple voltage to HX711 Load Amplifier Module. HX711 is a 24bit ADC, which intensifies and changes over the Load cell yield into advanced structure. At that point this intensified worth is bolstered to the Raspberry Pi. Presently Raspberry Pi figures the yield of HX711 and changes over that into the weight esteem. At that point Raspberry Pi contrasts the worth and reference weight and drives the door appropriately by utilizing engine driver IC L293D. Here we have utilized DC engine for exhibit it as entryway. In the event that you need to utilize DVD Trolley as an entryway, at that point check our past instructional exercise: Automatic Door Opener utilizing Arduino

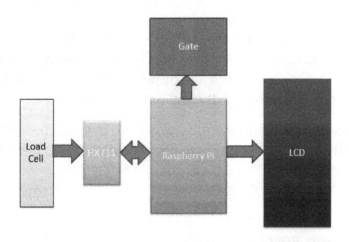

Here we have utilized Reference weight of 100 gram, implies in case somebody more noteworthy than 100gm will be remaining there close to the entryway, at that point just door will be opened. Furthermore, the entryway will shut when we expel that 100gm or the individual is no more. You can change the reference weight appropriately. A discretionary 16x2

LCD is utilized for showing entryway status. We have composed a Python program for entire procedure, check the Python Code toward the finish of this instructional exercise.

Programming Explanation:

Here we have utilized Python for the Programming. In this undertaking, we didn't utilize any library for interfacing HX711 load sensor with Raspberry Pi. We have quite recently pursued the datasheet of HX711 and application notes. Despite the fact that there are a few libraries present for this reason, where you just need to incorporate that library and you can get the weight utilizing hardly any lines of code.

As a matter of first importance, we have included Library for GPIO sticks and characterized pins for LCD, HX711 as well as DC engine, likewise pronounced a few factors for count reason.

```
import RPi.GPIO as gpio

import time

RS = 18

EN = 23
```

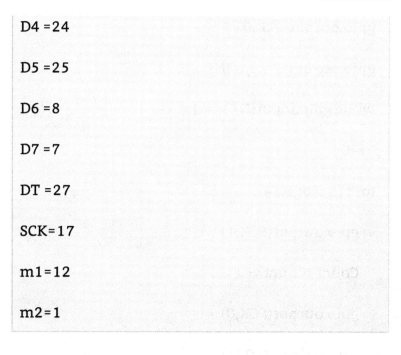

```
D4 = 24

D5 = 25

D6 = 8

D7 = 7

DT = 27

SCK = 17

m1 = 12

m2 = 1
```

After it, we have made beneath work for perusing information from HX711 module and return its yield.

```
def readCount():

  i=0

  Count=0

  gpio.setup(DT, gpio.OUT)

  gpio.output(DT,1)
```

```
gpio.output(SCK,0)

gpio.setup(DT, gpio.IN)

while gpio.input(DT) == 1:

  i=0

for i in range(24):

   gpio.output(SCK,1)

   Count=Count<<1

   gpio.output(SCK,0)

   #time.sleep(0.001)

     if gpio.input(DT) == 0:

     Count=Count+1

gpio.output(SCK,1)

Count=Count^0x800000

gpio.output(SCK,0)

 return Count
```

New in fundamental capacity, we read information from HX711 module and contrast it and reference weight and take activities to open or close the door in like manner.

```
while 1:

  count = readCount()

  w = 0

  w = (count-sample)/106

  print w,"g"

  if w > 100:

    setCursor(0,0)

    lcdprint("Gate Opened ")

    if flag == 0:

      gpio.output(m1, 1)

      gpio.output(m2, 0)

      time.sleep(1.3)
```

```
        gpio.output(m1, 0)

        gpio.output(m2, 0)

        time.sleep(1.5)

        flag=1;

        lcdclear()

   elif w<100:

      setCursor(0,0)

      lcdprint("Gate Closed ")

      if flag==1:

        gpio.output(m1, 0)

        gpio.output(m2, 1)

        time.sleep(1.3)

        gpio.output(m1, 0)

        gpio.output(m2, 0)

        time.sleep(2)
```

```
    flag=0

  time.sleep(0.5)
```

A few capacities are additionally made for LCD, as def start(): for introduce the LCD, def lcdcmd(ch): for sending directions to LCD, def lcdwrite(ch): for printing character on LCD, def lcdclear(): for clearing the LCD and def lcdprint(Str): for printing the string. Check every one of the capacities in the Full code given beneath.

Here we had seen that we can without much of a stretch make this Weight detecting Automatic Gate utilizing Raspberry Pi and Load cell.

Code

```
import RPi.GPIO as gpio
import time

RS =18
EN =23
D4 =24
D5 =25
D6 =8
D7 =7

DT =27
SCK=17

m1=12
```

```
m2=16

HIGH=1
LOW=0

sample=0
val=0

gpio.setwarnings(False)
gpio.setmode(gpio.BCM)
gpio.setup(RS, gpio.OUT)
gpio.setup(EN, gpio.OUT)
gpio.setup(D4, gpio.OUT)
gpio.setup(D5, gpio.OUT)
gpio.setup(D6, gpio.OUT)
gpio.setup(D7, gpio.OUT)
gpio.setup(m1, gpio.OUT)
gpio.setup(m2, gpio.OUT)
gpio.setup(SCK, gpio.OUT)
gpio.output(m1 , 0)
gpio.output(m2 , 0)

defbegin():
 lcdcmd(0x33)
 lcdcmd(0x32)
 lcdcmd(0x06)
 lcdcmd(0x0C)
 lcdcmd(0x28)
 lcdcmd(0x01)
 time.sleep(0.0005)


deflcdcmd(ch):
```

```
gpio.output(RS, 0)
gpio.output(D4, 0)
gpio.output(D5, 0)
gpio.output(D6, 0)
gpio.output(D7, 0)
if ch&0x10==0x10:
 gpio.output(D4, 1)
if ch&0x20==0x20:
 gpio.output(D5, 1)
if ch&0x40==0x40:
 gpio.output(D6, 1)
if ch&0x80==0x80:
 gpio.output(D7, 1)
gpio.output(EN, 1)
time.sleep(0.005)
gpio.output(EN, 0)

# Low bits
gpio.output(D4, 0)
gpio.output(D5, 0)
gpio.output(D6, 0)
gpio.output(D7, 0)
if ch&0x01==0x01:
 gpio.output(D4, 1)
if ch&0x02==0x02:
 gpio.output(D5, 1)
if ch&0x04==0x04:
 gpio.output(D6, 1)
if ch&0x08==0x08:
 gpio.output(D7, 1)
gpio.output(EN, 1)
```

```
time.sleep(0.005)
gpio.output(EN, 0)


deflcdwrite(ch):
gpio.output(RS, 1)
gpio.output(D4, 0)
gpio.output(D5, 0)
gpio.output(D6, 0)
gpio.output(D7, 0)
if ch&0x10==0x10:
 gpio.output(D4, 1)
if ch&0x20==0x20:
 gpio.output(D5, 1)
if ch&0x40==0x40:
 gpio.output(D6, 1)
if ch&0x80==0x80:
 gpio.output(D7, 1)
gpio.output(EN, 1)
time.sleep(0.005)
gpio.output(EN, 0)

# Low bits
gpio.output(D4, 0)
gpio.output(D5, 0)
gpio.output(D6, 0)
gpio.output(D7, 0)
if ch&0x01==0x01:
 gpio.output(D4, 1)
if ch&0x02==0x02:
 gpio.output(D5, 1)
```

```
if ch&0x04==0x04:
  gpio.output(D6, 1)
if ch&0x08==0x08:
  gpio.output(D7, 1)
gpio.output(EN, 1)
time.sleep(0.005)
gpio.output(EN, 0)

def lcdclear():
lcdcmd(0x01)


def lcdprint(Str):
l=0;
l=len(Str)
for i in range(l):
  lcdwrite(ord(Str[i]))


def setCursor(x,y):
  if y == 0:
    n=128+x
  elif y == 1:
    n=192+x
  lcdcmd(n)

def readCount():
i=0
Count=0
# print Count
# time.sleep(0.001)
gpio.setup(DT, gpio.OUT)
```

```python
gpio.output(DT,1)
gpio.output(SCK,0)
gpio.setup(DT, gpio.IN)

while gpio.input(DT) == 1:
  i=0
for i in range(24):
    gpio.output(SCK,1)
    Count=Count<<1

    gpio.output(SCK,0)
    #time.sleep(0.001)
    if gpio.input(DT) == 0:
      Count=Count+1
      #print Count


 gpio.output(SCK,1)
Count=Count^0x800000
#time.sleep(0.001)
gpio.output(SCK,0)
return Count

begin()
lcdcmd(0x01)
lcdprint(" Automatic Gate ")
lcdcmd(0xc0)
lcdprint("  Using RPI  ")
time.sleep(3)
lcdcmd(0x01)
lcdprint("Hello World")
lcdcmd(0xc0)
```

```
lcdprint("Welcomes You")
time.sleep(3)
sample= readCount()
flag=0
lcdclear()
while 1:
 count= readCount()
 w=0
 w=(count-sample)/106
 print w,"g"
 if w>100:
  setCursor(0,0)
  lcdprint("Gate Opened ")
  if flag == 0:
   gpio.output(m1, 1)
   gpio.output(m2, 0)
   time.sleep(1.3)
   gpio.output(m1, 0)
   gpio.output(m2, 0)
   time.sleep(1.5)
   flag=1;
   lcdclear()
 elif w<100:
  setCursor(0,0)
  lcdprint("Gate Closed ")
  if flag==1:
   gpio.output(m1, 0)
   gpio.output(m2, 1)
   time.sleep(1.3)
   gpio.output(m1, 0)
```

```
gpio.output(m2, 0)
time.sleep(2)
flag=0
time.sleep(0.5)
```

◆ ◆ ◆

3. RASPBERRY PI EMERGENCY LIGHT WITH DARKNESS AS WELL AS ALTERNATING CURRENT POWER LINE OFF DETECTOR

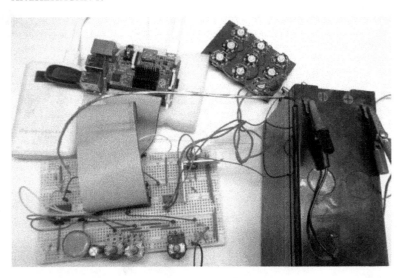

We are going to make a 9 WATT Emergency Lamp utilizing Raspberry Pi as well as Python. This light will naturally recognize the obscurity and nonattendance of AC control supply, and light up when there is control disappointment and appropriate light isn't there.

Despite the fact that there are different crisis lights accessible however they are absolutely devoted to fill single need, similar to one Simple Emergency Light Circuit that we have made already, triggers just on control disappointment. With Raspberry Pi we can add different functionalities to it, as here we have added LDR to distinguish Darkness at different levels. Here we have included two levels, when there is finished dim, the light will gleam with full power and when there is semi dim, it will shine at 30% limit. We are gonna to plan this light to be turned ON when AC line control is OFF and when the light power in the room goes exceptionally low.

Components Required:

Here we are utilizing Raspberry Pi 2 Model B with Raspbian Jessie OS. All the essential Hardware and Software necessities are recently talked about, you can find it in the Raspberry Pi Introduction and Raspberry PI LED Blinking for beginning, other than that we need:

- 1000µF capacitor
- 1 WATT LED (9 pieces)
- +12V Sealed LEAD ACID battery
- 6000-10000mAH power bank
- +5V DC adapter
- Lm324 OP-AMP chip
- 4N25 Optocoupler
- IRFZ44N MOSFET
- LDR (Light Dependent Resistor)
- LED (1 piece)
- Resistors: 1K? (3 pieces), 2.2K?, 4.7K?, 100? (2 pieces), 10? (9 pieces), 10K?, 100K?
- 10K? pot (3 pieces) (all resistors are 0.25 watt)

Description:

Prior to going into Circuit Connections and its working, we will find out about the segments and their motivation in the circuit:

9 Watt Light Emitting Diode Lamp:

The LAMP is comprised of nine 1WATT LEDs. There are various types of LEDs present in advertise yet 1WATT LED are effectively accessible all over the place. These LED work at 3.6V, so we will interface three of them in arrangement alongside insurance diodes to work at +12V. We will associate three of these strips framing a 9WATT LED light. We will work this light with Raspberry Pi appropriately.

(Light Dependent Resistor) to identify Darkness:

We are going to utilize (Light Dependent Resistor) to identify the light force in the room. The Light Dependent Resistor changes its opposition directly with the light power. This LDR will be associated with voltage divider. With that we will have variable voltage to speak to variable light force. In case the light force is LOW the voltage yield will be HIGH and if light power if HIGH voltage yield will be LOW.

Operation amp LM324 IC for checking LDR yield:

Raspberry Pi doesn't have an inner ADC (Analog to Digital Converter) system. So this arrangement can't be associated legitimately to Raspberry Pi. We will utilize OP-AMP based comparators to check the voltage yields from LDR.

Here we have utilized operation amp LM324 which has four operational enhancers inside it and we have utilized two operation amps out of those four. So our PI will have the option to distinguish light force at two levels. Contingent upon these levels we will modify the splendor of LED light. When there is finished dim, the light will shine with full force and when there is half dull, it will gleam at 30% limit. Check the Python code toward the end, to comprehend it appropriately. Here we have utilized PWM idea in Raspberry Pi to manage the power of LEDs.

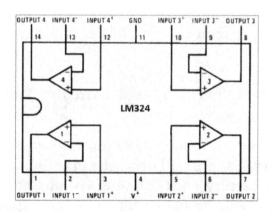

Raspberry Pi has 26GPIO, out of which some are utilized for exceptional capacities. With extraordinary GPIO set aside, we have 17 GPIO. Every one of the 17 GPIO pins can't take voltage higher than +3.3V, so the Op-amp yields can't be higher than 3.3V. Subsequently we have picked operation amp LM324, as this chip can work at +3.3V giving rationale yields not more than +3.3V. Study GPIO Pins of Raspberry Pi here. Additionally check our Raspberry Pi Tutorial Series alongside some great IoT Projects.

Air conditioning to DC Adapter to check the AC Line:

We will utilize AC to DC connector outlet voltage rationale to identify the AC line status. In case there are many methods to recognize the AC line status, this is the most secure and least demanding approach. We will take +5V rationale from connector and offer it to Raspberry Pi through a voltage divider circuit to clandestine +5V high rationale to +3.3v HIGH rationale. See the circuit chart for better understanding.

Power Bank and 12v Lead corrosive Battery for Power Supply:

Remember that Raspberry Pi must be working without control, so we will drive the PI utilizing a Power Bank (A battery pack 10000mAH) and the 9WATT LED light will be fueled by +12V, 7AH fixed LEAD ACID battery. The LED light can't be controlled by control bank as they draw a lot of intensity, so they should be fueled from a different power source.

You can control the Raspberry Pi by +12V battery in

the event that you have an effective +12V to +5v converter. By that converter you can dump the power bank as well as power the whole circuit with a solitary battery source.

Circuit Explanation:

Circuit Diagram of Raspberry Pi Emergency Light is given beneath:

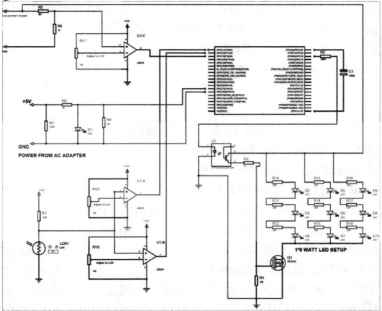

Here we have utilized three out of four comparator inside LM324 IC. Two of them will be utilized to identify light power levels and the third one will be utilized to recognize the low voltage level of +12V battery.

1. Operation AMP1 otherwise U1A: -ve terminal of this comparator is furnished with 1.2V (modify RV2 to get the voltage) and Positive terminal is associated with LDR voltage divider organize. As the shade falls on the LDR, its inward opposition rises. With the ascent in inner obstruction of LDR, the voltage drop at the +ve terminal of OP-AMP1 rises. When this voltage goes higher than 1.2V, the OP-AMP1 gives +3.3V yield. This HIGH rationale yield of OP-AMP will be identified by Raspberry Pi.

2. Operation AMP2 or U1B: Negative terminal of this comparator is furnished with 2.2V (modify RV3 to get the voltage) and Positive terminal is associated with LDR voltage divider organize. As the shade falling on the LDR further builds, its inner opposition goes much higher. With further ascent in inward obstruction of LDR, the voltage drop at the +ve terminal of OP-AMP2 rises. When this voltage goes higher than 2.2V, the OP-AMP2 gives +3.3V yield. This HIGH rationale yield of OP-AMP will be recognized by Raspberry Pi.

3. Operation AMP3 otherwise U1C: This OP-AMP will be utilized to distinguish low voltage level of +12v battery pack. -ve terminal of this comparator is furnished with 2.1V (alter RV1to get the voltage) and positive terminal is associated with a voltage divider circuit. This divider partitions the battery voltage by 1/5.7 occasions, along these lines for 12.5V battery voltage we will have 2.19V at the +ve terminal of OP-AMP3. At the point when battery voltage goes underneath 12.0V, voltage at positive terminal will be <2.1V. So with the 2.1v at negative terminal, OP-AMP yield goes low. So when battery voltage dips under 12V (implies beneath 2.1v at positive terminal), the OP-AMP pulls down the yield, this rationale will be recognized by Raspberry Pi.

Working Explanation:

The entire capacity of this Raspberry Pi Emergency Lamp can de expressed as:

First Raspberry Pi distinguishes if there is AC control present or not by detecting rationale at GPIO23, where +3.3V from Alternating Current connector is taken. When the power goes OFF, +5V from connector goes OFF and Raspberry Pi goes to the following stage just if this LOW rationale is identified, if not PI won't move to subsequent stage. This LOW rationale happens just when AC control goes OFF.

Next PI checks if the LEAD ACID battery level is LOW. This rationale is given by OP-AMP3 at GPIO16. In case the rationale is LOW, at that point PI doesn't move to subsequent stage. With battery voltage higher than +12V, PI moves to following stage.

Next Raspberry Pi checks if the haziness in the room is HIGH, this rationale is given by OP-AMP2 at GPIO20. In case indeed, PI gives (Pulse Width Modulation) yield with an obligation cycle of 99%. This Pulse Width Modulation signal drives the opto-coupler which drives the MOSFET. MOSFET powers the 9 WATT Light Emitting Diode arrangement as appeared in figure. On the off chance that there isn't finished dim, at that point PI moves to following stage. Get familiar with PWM in Raspberry Pi here.

At that point Raspberry Pi checks if the haziness in the room is LOW, this rationale is given by OP-AMP1 at GPIO21. In the event that indeed, PI gives (Pulse Width Modulation) yield with an obligation cycle of 30%. This Pulse Width Modulation signal drives the opto-coupler which drives the MOSFET. MOSFET powers the 9 WATT Light Emitting Diode arrangement as appeared in figure. In the event that there is appropriate light in the room, at that point Raspberry Pi doesn't give PWM yield so the LAMP will be totally OFF.

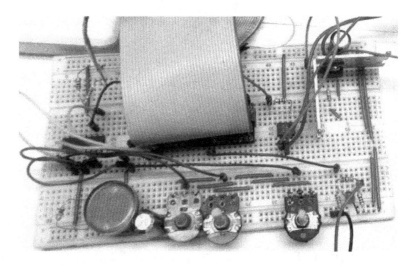

So to turn on this Emergency Lamp, both the condition must be True, implies AC line must be off and there must be haziness in the room. You can get the unmistakable comprehension by checking the total Python Code beneath.

You can additionally include all the more intriguing functionalities and haziness levels to this Emergency light. Additionally check our more Power Electronics circuits:

- 0-24v 3A Variable Power Supply utilizing LM338

- 12v Battery Charger Circuit utilizing LM317

- 12v Direct Current to 220v AC Inverter Circuit

- Mobile phone Charger Circuit

Code

```
import RPi.GPIO as IO    #calling for header file which
helps in using GPIOs of PI
import time
IO.setwarnings(False)    #do not show any warnings
IO.setmode (IO.BCM)      #programming the GPIO by
BCM pin numbers

IO.setup(19,IO.OUT)    #initialize GPIO19 as an out-
put
IO.setup(21,IO.IN)     #initialize GPIO21,20,16,12,23
as inputs
IO.setup(20,IO.IN)
IO.setup(16,IO.IN)
IO.setup(12,IO.IN)
IO.setup(23,IO.IN)

p = IO.PWM(19,200)    #GPIO19 is set as PWM output
with frequency at 200Hz
p.start(1)      #start PWM output with 1% duty cycle

while 1:
  if(IO.input(23) == False):   #If AC power is OFF
   if(IO.input(16) == True): #If battery voltage > +12V
    if (IO.input(20) == True):   #If its complete dark
      time.sleep(0.01)
     if(IO.input(20) == True):   #If its complete dark
        p.ChangeDutyCycle(99) #change PWM duty
cycle to 99%
     elif(IO.input(21) == True):   #else If its semi dark
```

```
       time.sleep(0.01)
       if(IO.input(21) == True):   #else If its semi dark
           p.ChangeDutyCycle(30) #change PWM duty
cycle to 30%
       elif(IO.input(21) == False):   #if its not even semi
dark
       time.sleep(0.01)
       if(IO.input(21) == False):
           p.ChangeDutyCycle(0)   #turn OFF the LAMP
       time.sleep(0.1)
    if(IO.input(23) == True):   #If AC power is ON
       p.ChangeDutyCycle(0)   #turn OFF the LAMP
    if(IO.input(16) == False):   #If battery voltage < +12V
       p.ChangeDutyCycle(0)   #turn OFF the LAMP
```

◆ ◆ ◆

4. RECOGNIZING COLORS UTILIZING RASPBERRY PI AND COLOR SENSOR TCS3200

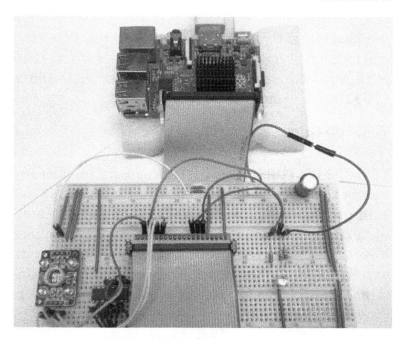

In this task we will Detect the Colors utilizing TCS3200 Color Sensor Module with Raspberry Pi. Here we utilized Python code for Raspberry Pi to recognize the hues utilizing TCS3200 sensor. To show the shading discovery we have utilized a RGB LED, this RGB LED will shine in a similar shading, of which the article is displayed close to the sensor. At present we have customized Raspberry Pi to recognize just Red, Green as well as blue hues. Yet, you can program it to identify any shading in the wake of getting the RGB esteems, as each shading is comprised of these RGB parts.

We have recently perused and shown the RGB estimations of the hues utilizing the equivalent TCS3200 with Arduino. Before going any further, tells about TCS3200 Color Sensor.

TCS3200 Color Sensor:

TCS3200 is a Color Sensor which can distinguish any number of hues with right programming. TCS3200 contains RGB (Red Green Blue) clusters. As appeared in figure on minuscule level, one can see the square boxes inside the eye on sensor. These square boxes are varieties of RGB framework. Each of these cases contains three sensors for detecting Red, Green as well as Blue light power.

So we have Red, Blue and Green exhibits on same layer. So while distinguishing shading we can't recognize each of the three components at the same time. Each and every sensors clusters are to be chosen independently in a steady progression to recognize the shading. The module can be customized to detect the specific shading and to leave the others. It contains pins for that determination reason, which has been clarified later. There is forward mode that is no channel mode; with no channel mode the sensor identifies white light.

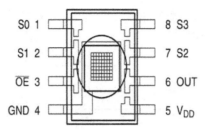

We will associate this sensor to Raspberry Pi and will program the Raspberry Pi to give fitting reaction relying upon shading.

Components Required:

Here we are utilizing Raspberry Pi 2 Model B with Raspbian Jessie OS. All the fundamental Hardware and Software prerequisites are recently talked about, you can find it in the Raspberry Pi Introduction and Raspberry PI LED Blinking for beginning, other than that we need:

- Raspberry Pi with pre-installed OS
- CD4040 counter chip
- TCS3200 color sensor
- 1K? resistor (three pieces)
- RGB LED
- 1000uF capacitor

Circuit Diagram and Connections:

The associations which are accomplished for interfacing the Color Sensor with Raspberry Pi are given in beneath table:

Sensor Pins	Raspberry Pi Pins
Vcc	+3.3v
GND	ground
S0	+3.3v
S1	+3.3v
S2	GPIO6 of PI
S3	GPIO5 of PI
OE	GPIO22 of PI
OUT	CLK of CD4040

The associations for CD4040 counter with Raspberry Pi are given in underneath table:

CD4040 Pins	Raspberry Pi Pins

Vcc16	+3.3v
Gnd8	gnd
Clk10	OUT of sensor
Reset11	GPIO26 of PI
Q0	GPIO21 of PI
Q1	GPIO20 of PI
Q2	GPIO16 of PI
Q3	GPIO12 of PI
Q4	GPIO25 of PI
Q5	GPIO24 of PI
Q6	GPIO23 of PI
Q7	GPIO18 of PI
Q8	No connection
Q9	No connection

Q10	No connection
Q11	No connection

The following is the full circuit chart of Interfacing Color Sensor with Raspberry Pi:

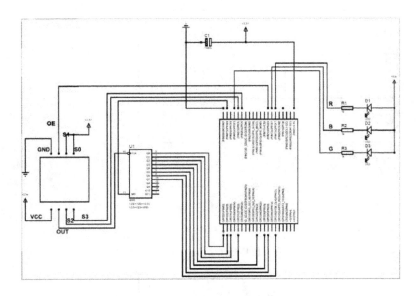

Working Explanation:

Each shading is comprised of three hues: (RGB). Furthermore, in case we know the powers of RGB in any shading, at that point we can recognize that shading. We have recently perused these RGB esteems utilizing

Arduino.

Utilizing TCS3200 Color Sensor, we can't recognize RGB light simultaneously so we have to check them individually. The shading which should be detected by the Color Sensor is chosen by two pins S2 as well as S3. With these two pins, we can tell the sensor which shading light power is to be estimated.

State in the event that we have to detect the Red shading force, at that point we have to set the two pins to LOW. In the wake of getting the RED light estimated, we will set S2 LOW and S3 HIGH to quantify the blue light. By consecutively changing the rationales of S2 and S3 we can quantify Red, Blue and Green light powers, as per the underneath given table:

S2	S3	Photodiode Type
Low	Low	Red
Low	High	Blue
High	Low	No filter (white)
High	High	Green

When the sensor recognizes the forces of RGB segments, the worth is sent to the control framework inside the module as appeared in the figure underneath. The light power estimated by cluster is sent to the Current to Frequency converter inside the module. The recurrence converter creates a square wave whose recurrence is straightforwardly corresponding to the worth sent by the cluster. With higher incentive from the ARRAY, Current to Frequency converter creates the square influx of higher recurrence.

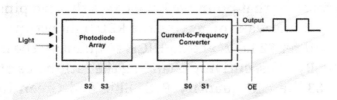

The yield signal recurrence by the shading sensor module can be changed in accordance with four levels. These levels are chosen by utilizing S0 and S1 of sensor module as appeared in underneath figure.

SO	S1	Output Frequency Scaling (f0)
L	L	Power Down
L	H	2%
H	L	20%

H	H	100%

This component proves to be useful when we are interfacing this module to the framework with low clock. With Raspberry Pi we will choose 100%. Recollect here, under the shade the Color Sensor Module creates a square wave yield whose greatest recurrence is 2500Hz (100% scaling) for each shading.

In case the module gives yield square wave whose recurrence is in straightforwardly extent to light power falling on its surface, there is no simple method to ascertain the light force of each shading by this module. Anyway we can tell whether the light power is expanding or diminishing for each shading. Likewise we can compute and think about the Red, Green, Blue qualities to recognize the shade of light or shade of article preset at the outside of module. So this is a greater amount of Color Sensor module instead of Light Intensity Sensor module.

Presently we will sustain this Square wave yield to the Raspberry Pi yet we can't give it straightforwardly to PI, since Raspberry Pi doesn't have any inward counters. So first we will give this yield to CD4040 Binary Counter and we will program Raspberry Pi to take the recurrence esteem from the counter at intermittent interims of 100msec.

So the PI peruses an estimation of 2500/10 = 250 max for every RED, GREEN and BLUE shading. We have additionally customized Raspberry Pi to print these qualities speaking to the light forces on the screen as demonstrated as follows. The qualities are subtracted from the default esteems to reach to zero. This proves to be useful while choosing the shading.

Here the default esteems are the estimations of RGB, which have taken without setting any article before sensor. It relies on the encompassing light conditions and these qualities can varies as per environment. Fundamentally we are aligning the sensor for standard readings. So first run the program without putting any article and note the readings. These qualities won't be almost zero as there will be in every case some light falling on the sensor regardless of where you place it. At that point subtract those readings with the readings which we will get in the wake of putting an item to test. Thusly we can get standard readings.

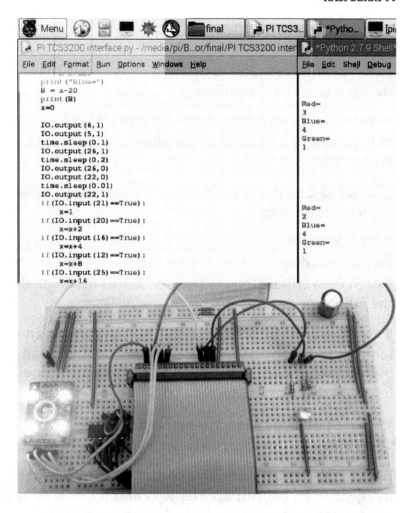

Raspberry Pi is likewise customized to think about the R, G and B esteems to decide the shade of the item set close to the sensor. This outcome is appeared by sparkling RGB LED associated with Raspberry Pi.

So in nutshell,

1. The module recognizes the light reflected by the article put close to the surface.

2. The Color Sensor Module gives yield wave to R or G or B, picked successively by Raspberry Pi through the Pins S2 and S3.

3. CD4040 Counter takes the wave and measures the recurrence esteem.

4. PI takes the recurrence esteem from the counter for each shading for each 100ms. After the taking the worth each time PI resets the counter to distinguish the following worth.

5. Raspberry Pi prints these qualities on screen and looks at these qualities to distinguish the item shading lastly gleam the RGB LED in suitable shading relying upon shade of article.

We have pursued the above succession in our Python Code. Full program is given beneath.

Here Raspberry Pi is modified to distinguish just three hues, you can coordinate the R, G and B esteems as needs be to recognize more shades of your enjoying.

Code

#working

```
import time
import RPi.GPIO as IO

IO.setmode (IO.BCM)
IO.setwarnings(False) #do not show any warnings

x=0
IO.setup(6,IO.OUT    #pins 6,5,... are set as output
IO.setup(5,IO.OUT)
IO.setup(27,IO.OUT)
IO.setup(17,IO.OUT)
IO.setup(13,IO.OUT)
IO.setup(22,IO.OUT)
IO.setup(26,IO.OUT)

IO.setup(21,IO.IN)   #pins 21,20... are set as input
IO.setup(20,IO.IN)
IO.setup(16,IO.IN)
IO.setup(12,IO.IN)
IO.setup(25,IO.IN)
IO.setup(24,IO.IN)
IO.setup(23,IO.IN)
IO.setup(18,IO.IN)

while 1:
  IO.output(6,0)   #choose red array by putting S2 and
S3 low
  IO.output(5,0)
  time.sleep(0.1)
  IO.output(26,1)  #reset counter one time
  time.sleep(0.2)
  IO.output(26,0)
    IO.output(22,0)    #enable output of module for
```

100msec for counter to read frequency

```
time.sleep(0.01)
IO.output(22,1)
if(IO.input(21)==True):
  x=1
if(IO.input(20)==True):
  x=x+2
if(IO.input(16)==True):
  x=x+4
if(IO.input(12)==True):
  x=x+8
if(IO.input(25)==True):
  x=x+16
if(IO.input(24)==True):
  x=x+32
if(IO.input(23)==True):
  x=x+64
if(IO.input(18)==True):
  x=x+128
print("Red=")   #detect value counted by counter
R = x-50
print(R)
x=0


  IO.output(6,0)   #choose blue array
IO.output(5,1)
time.sleep(0.1)
IO.output(26,1)  #reset counter one time
time.sleep(0.2)
IO.output(26,0)
```

```
    IO.output(22,0)    #enable output of module for
100msec for counter to read frequency
  time.sleep(0.01)
  IO.output(22,1)
  if(IO.input(21)==True):
    x=1
  if(IO.input(20)==True):
    x=x+2
  if(IO.input(16)==True):
    x=x+4
  if(IO.input(12)==True):
    x=x+8
  if(IO.input(25)==True):
    x=x+16
  if(IO.input(24)==True):
    x=x+32
  if(IO.input(23)==True):
    x=x+64
  if(IO.input(18)==True):
    x=x+128
  print("Blue=")   #detect value counted by counter
  B = x-20
  print(B)
  x=0


    IO.output(6,1)   #choose green array
  IO.output(5,1)
  time.sleep(0.1)
  IO.output(26,1)  #reset counter one time
  time.sleep(0.2)
```

```
IO.output(26,0)
 IO.output(22,0)    #enable output of module for
100msec for counter to read frequency
 time.sleep(0.01)
 IO.output(22,1)
 if(IO.input(21)==True):
   x=1
 if(IO.input(20)==True):
   x=x+2
 if(IO.input(16)==True):
   x=x+4
 if(IO.input(12)==True):
   x=x+8
 if(IO.input(25)==True):
   x=x+16
 if(IO.input(24)==True):
   x=x+32
 if(IO.input(23)==True):
   x=x+64
 if(IO.input(18)==True):
   x=x+128
 print("Green=")  #detect value counted by counter
 G=x-42
 print(G)
 x=0
 print
 print
 print
 print
 print
```

```
print

    if((R>=B+10)and(R>=G+10)):   #if RED color inten-
sity is high light RED led
      IO.output(17,0)
    elif((G>=B+10)and(G>=R+10)): #if GREEN color in-
tensity is high light GREEN led
      IO.output(13,0)
    elif((B>=R+10)and(B>=G+10)): #if BLUE color in-
tensity is high light BLUE led
      IO.output(27,0)


    time.sleep(2)   #after 2 sec turn off LEDs
   IO.output(17,1)
   IO.output(13,1)
   IO.output(27,1)
```

◆ ◆ ◆

5. MEASURE DISTANCE UTILIZING RASPBERRY PI AND HCSR04 ULTRASONIC SENSOR

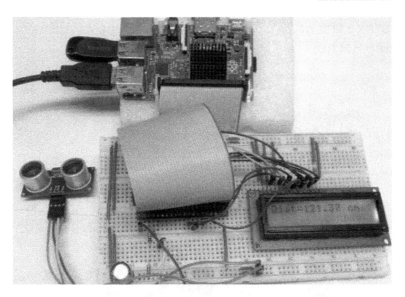

We are gonna to interface HC-SR04 US Sensor module to Raspberry Pi to quantify separation. We have recently utilized Ultrasonic sensor with Raspberry Pi to assemble Obstacle Avoiding Robot. Before going any further, tells about US sensor.

HC-SR04 Ultrasonic Sensor:

The US Sensor is used to quantify the separation with high precision as well as stable readings. It can gauge good ways from two cm to four hundred cm otherwise from one inch to thirteen feet. It produces a ultrasound wave at the recurrence of 40KHz noticeable all around and in the event that the item will come in its manner, at that point it will skip back to the sensor. By utilizing that time which it takes to strike the article and returns, you can ascertain the separation.

The ultrasonic sensor utilizes a procedure called "Reverberation". "Reverberation" is essentially a reflected sound wave. You will have an ECHO when sound reflects back in the wake of arriving at an impasse.

HCSR04 module creates a sound vibration in us range when we make the 'Trigger' pin high for about ten us which will send a eight cycle sonic burst at the speed of sound and in case of striking the article, it will be gotten by the Echo pin. Contingent upon time taken by sound vibration to get back, it gives fitting heartbeat yield. In the event that the item is far away, at that point it requires some investment for ECHO to be heard and the yield beat width will be large. Also, in case the impediment is close, at that point the ECHO will be heard quicker and yield beat width will be littler.

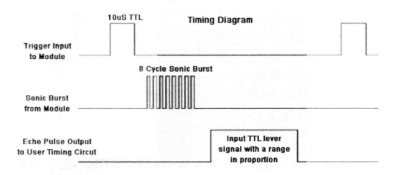

We can compute the separation of the item dependent on the time taken by ultrasonic wave to return back to the sensor. Since the time and speed of sound is realized we can compute the separation by the accompanying formulae.

- Distance= (Time x Speed of Sound in Air (343 m/s))/2.

The worth is isolated by two since the wave goes ahead and in reverse covering the equivalent distance.Thus an opportunity to arrive at snag is simply a large portion of the complete time taken

So Distance in centimeter = 17150*T

We have recently made numerous helpful venture

utilizing this Ultrasonic sensor and Arduino, check them underneath:

- Arduino Based Distance Measurement utilizing Ultrasonic Sensor
- Entryway Alarm utilizing Arduino as well as US Sensor
- IOT Based Dumpster Monitoring utilizing Arduino

Components Required:

Here we are utilizing Raspberry Pi 2 Model B with Raspbian Jessie OS. All the essential Hardware and Software necessities are recently talked about, you can find it in the Raspberry Pi Introduction and Raspberry PI LED Blinking for beginning, other than that we need:

- Raspberry Pi with pre-installed OS
- HC-SR04 US Sensor
- Power supply (5v)
- 1K? resistor (3 pieces)
- 1000uF capacitor
- 16*2 character LCD

Circuit Explanation:

Associations between Raspberry Pi and LCD are given

in the beneath table:

LCD connection	Raspberry Pi connection
GND	GND
VCC	+5V
VEE	GND
RS	GPIO17
R/W	GND
EN	GPIO27
D0	GPIO24
D1	GPIO23
D2	GPIO18
D3	GPIO26
D4	GPIO5
D5	GPIO6

D6	GPIO13
D7	GPIO19

In this circuit, we utilized 8bit correspondence (D0-D7) to associate LCD with Raspberry Pi, anyway this is certifiably not an obligatory, we can likewise utilize 4-piece correspondence (D4-D7), yet with 4 piece correspondence program turns into somewhat complex for apprentices so simply go with 8 piece correspondence. Here we have associated ten pins of LCD to Raspberry Pi in which eight pins are information pins as well as 2 pins are control Pins.

The following is the circuit chart for associating HC-SR04 sensor and LCD with Raspberry Pi for estimating the separation.

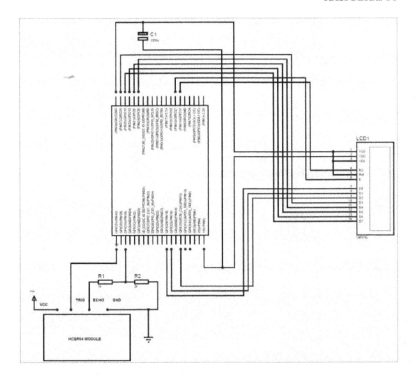

As appeared in the figure, HC-SR04 Ultrasonic Sensor has four pins,

- PIN1-VCC or +5V

- PIN2-TRIGGER (10us High heartbeat given to advise the sensor to detect the separation)

- PIN3-ECHO (Provides beat yield whose width speaks to separate after trigger)

- PIN4-GROUND

Reverberation pin gives +5V yield beat which can't be associated with Raspberry Pi legitimately. So we will utilize Voltage Divider Circuit (constructed utilizing R1 and R2) to get +3.3V rationale rather than +5V rationale.

Working Explanation:

Complete working of Raspberry Pi Distance Measure goes as,

1. Setting off the sensor by pulling up the trigger pin for 10uS.

2. Sound wave is sent by the sensor. Subsequent to getting the ECHO, sensor module gives a yield corresponding to separate.

3. We will record when the yield beat goes from LOW to HIGH and when again when its goes structure HIGH to LOW.

4. We will have start and stop time. We will utilize separation condition to figure the separation.

5. The separation is shown in 16x2 LCD show.

As needs be we have composed the Python Program for Raspberry Pi to do the accompanying capacities:

1. To send trigger to sensor

2. Record start and prevent time of heartbeat yield from sensor.

3. To Calculate the separation by utilizing START and STOP time.

4. To Display the outcome acquired on the 16*2 LCD.

Complete Program is given underneath. Program is all around clarified through the remarks.

Code

```
import time
import RPi.GPIO as IO   #calling for header file which helps in using GPIOs of PI

string_of_characters = 0

IO.setwarnings(False)   #do not show any warnings
IO.setmode (IO.BCM)      #programming the GPIO by BCM pin numbers. (like PIN29 as GPIO5)
IO.setup(17,IO.OUT)                      #initialize GPIO17,27,24,23,18,26,5,6,13,19,21 as an output
IO.setup(27,IO.OUT)
IO.setup(24,IO.OUT)
IO.setup(23,IO.OUT)
IO.setup(18,IO.OUT)
IO.setup(26,IO.OUT)
IO.setup(5,IO.OUT)
IO.setup(6,IO.OUT)
IO.setup(13,IO.OUT)
```

```
IO.setup(19,IO.OUT)
IO.setup(21,IO.OUT)
IO.setup(16,IO.IN)    #initialize GPIO16 as an input

def send_a_command (command): #steps for sending
a command to 16x2 LCD
  pin=command
  PORT(pin);
  IO.output(17,0)
  #PORTD&= ~(1<<RS);
  IO.output(27,1)
  #PORTD|= (1<<E);
  time.sleep(0.001)
  #_delay_ms(50);
  IO.output(27,0)
  #PORTD&= ~(1<<E);
  pin=0
  PORT(pin);


def send_a_character (character): #steps for sending a
character to 16x2 LCD
  pin=character
  PORT(pin);
  IO.output(17,1)
  #PORTD|= (1<<RS);
  IO.output(27,1)
  #PORTD|= (1<<E);
  time.sleep(0.001)
  #_delay_ms(50);
  IO.output(27,0)
  #PORTD&= ~(1<<E);
```

```
pin=0
PORT(pin);
```

```python
def PORT(pin):          #assigning level for PI GPIO for
sending data to LCD through D0-D7
  if(pin&0x01 == 0x01):
    IO.output(24,1)
  else:
    IO.output(24,0)
  if(pin&0x02 == 0x02):
    IO.output(23,1)
  else:
    IO.output(23,0)
  if(pin&0x04 == 0x04):
    IO.output(18,1)
  else:
    IO.output(18,0)
  if(pin&0x08 == 0x08):
    IO.output(26,1)
  else:
    IO.output(26,0)
  if(pin&0x10 == 0x10):
    IO.output(5,1)
  else:
    IO.output(5,0)
  if(pin&0x20 == 0x20):
    IO.output(6,1)
  else:
    IO.output(6,0)
  if(pin&0x40 == 0x40):
    IO.output(13,1)
```

```
  else:
    IO.output(13,0)
  if(pin&0x80 == 0x80):
    IO.output(19,1)
  else:
    IO.output(19,0)

def send_a_string(string_of_characters):
    string_of_characters = string_of_characters.l-
just(16," ")
 for i in range(16):
      send_a_character(ord(string_of_characters[i]))
#send characters one by one through data port


while 1:
  send_a_command(0x38); #16x2 line LCD
  send_a_command(0x0E); #screen and cursor ON
  send_a_command(0x01); #clear screen
  time.sleep(0.1)        #sleep for 100msec


  IO.setup(21,1)
  time.sleep(0.00001)
  IO.setup(21,0)        #sending trigger pulse for sensor
to measure the distance


  while (IO.input(16)==0):
    start = time.time() #store the start time of pulse
output
```

```
while (IO.input(16)==1):
stop = time.time()  #store the stop time



    distance = ((stop - start)*17150)  #calculate dis-
tance from time
  distance = round(distance,2)    #round up the deci-
mal values
  if(distance<400):          #if distance is less than 400
cm, display the result on LCD
    send_a_command(0x80 + 0);
    send_a_string("Dist=%s cm"% (distance));
    time.sleep(0.15)


    if(distance>400):          #If distance is more than
400cm, just print 400+ on LCD
    send_a_command(0x80 + 0);
    send_a_string("Dist= 400+ cm");
    time.sleep(0.15)
```

◆ ◆ ◆

6. INTERFACING JOYSTICK WITH RASPBERRY PI

In this session we are going to Interface a Joystick with Raspberry Pi. Joystick is basically used to play different games. In spite of the fact that USB type joysticks are anything but difficult to interface, yet today we will associate Joystick through Raspberry Pi GPIO pins, this will prove to be useful as a rule.

Raspberry Pi and Joystick Module:

Joysticks are accessible in various shapes and sizes. A run of the mill Joystick module is appeared in the figure beneath. This Joystick module commonly gives Analog Outputs and the yield voltages gave by this module continue altering as per the course where we move it. Also, we can get the bearing of development by deciphering these voltage changes utilizing some microcontroller. Beforehand we have utilized AVR Microcontroller with Joystick.

This joystick module has two tomahawks as should be obvious. They are X-hub and Y-pivot. Every hub of JOY STICK is mounted to a potentiometer or pot. The mid purposes of these pots are driven out as Rx and Ry. So Rx and Ry are variable focuses to these pots. At the point when the Joystick is in backup, Rx and Ry go about as voltage divider.

At the point when joystick is moved along the even hub, the voltage at Rx pin changes. Essentially, when it is moved along the vertical hub, the voltage at Ry pin changes. So we have four headings of Joystick on two ADC yields. At the point when the stick is moved, the voltage on each pin goes high or low contingent upon course.

As we probably am aware Raspberry Pi doesn't have an inward ADC component. So this module can't be associated legitimately to the Pi. We will utilize Op-amp based comparators to check the voltage yields. These OP-Amps give sign to Raspberry Pi and Pi flips the LEDs to relying on the sign. Here we have utilized four LEDs to show the development of Joystick in four ways.

Every one of the 17 GPIO pins can't take voltage higher than +3.3V, so the Op-amp yields can't be higher than 3.3V. Subsequently we have picked operation amp LM324, this IC has quad operational enhancer which can work at 3V. With this IC, we have appropriate yields for yields for our Raspberry pi GPIO Pins. Get familiar with GPIO Pins of Raspberry Pi here. Additionally check our Raspberry Pi Tutorial Series alongside some great IoT Projects.

Components Required:

Here we are utilizing Raspberry Pi 2 Model B with Raspbian Jessie OS. All the essential Hardware and Software necessities are recently examined, you can find it in the Raspberry Pi Introduction and Raspberry PI LED Blinking for beginning, other than that we need:

- 1000µF capacitor
- Joystick Module

- LM324 Op-amp IC
- 1K? resistor (12 pieces)
- LED (4 pieces)
- 2.2K? resistor (4 pieces)

Circuit Diagram:

There are four OP-AMP comparators inside LM324 IC for identifying four headings of Joystick. The following is the outline of LM324 IC from its datasheet.

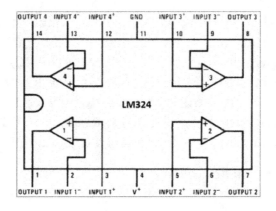

The associations which are accomplished for Interfacing Joystick module with Raspberry Pi are appeared in the circuit chart underneath. U1:A, U1:B, U1:C, U1:D shows the 4 comparators inside LM324. We have indicated each comparator in the circuit graph with the relating Pin no. of LM324 IC.

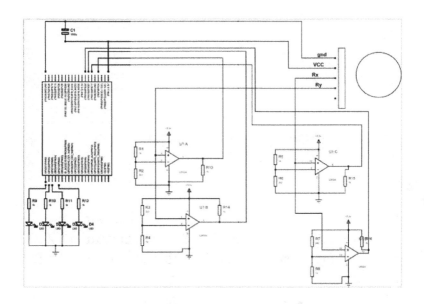

Working Explanation:

For recognizing the development of Joystick along the Y-hub, we have OP-AMP1 or U1:A and OP-AMP2 or U1:B, and for distinguishing the development of Joystick along the X-hub, we have OP-AMP3 or U1:C and OP-AMP4 or U1:D.

Operation AMP1 recognizes the drawback development of joystick along Y-hub:

Negative terminal of comparator U1:A is given 2.3V (utilizing voltage divider circuit by 1K and 2.2K) and

Positive terminal is associated with Ry. On moving the joystick down along its Y-pivot, Ry voltage increments. When this voltage goes higher than 2.3V, OP-AMP gives +3.3V yield at its yield Pin. This HIGH rationale yield of OP-AMP will be identified by Raspberry Pi and Pi reacts by flipping a LED.

Operation AMP2 distinguishes the upside development of joystick along Y-hub:

Negative terminal of comparator U1:B is furnished with 1.0V (utilizing voltage divider circuit by 2.2K and 1K) and Positive terminal is associated with Ry. On moving the joystick up along its Y-hub, Ry voltage diminishes. When this voltage goes lower than 1.0V, the OP-AMP yield goes Low. This LOW rationale yield of OP-AMP will be distinguished by Raspberry Pi and Pi reacts by flipping a LED.

Operation AMP3 identifies the left side development of joystick along X-hub:

-ve terminal of comparator U1:C is given 2.3V (utilizing voltage divider circuit by 1K and 2.2K) and Positive terminal is associated with Rx. On moving the joystick left along its x-hub, Rx voltage increments. When this voltage goes higher than 2.3V, OP-AMP gives +3.3V yield at its yield Pin. This HIGH rationale yield of OP-AMP will be recognized by Raspberry Pi and Pi reacts by flipping a LED.

Operation AMP4 recognizes the correct side development of joystick along X-pivot:

Negative terminal of comparator U1:4 is furnished with 1.0V (utilizing voltage divider circuit by 2.2K and 1K) and Positive terminal is associated with Rx. On moving the joystick directly along its x-hub, Rx voltage diminishes. When this voltage goes lower than 1.0V, the OP-AMP yield goes Low. This LOW rationale yield of OP-AMP will be recognized by Raspberry Pi and Pi reacts by flipping a LED.

Along these lines all the four rationales, which decide the four headings of Joystick, get associated with Raspberry Pi. Raspberry Pi takes the yields of these comparators as information sources and reacts in like manner by flipping the LEDs. The following are the outcomes appeared on the Raspberry Pi's terminal, as we have likewise printed the heading of Joystick on terminal utilizing our Python Code.

Python code is given underneath. Code is simple and can be comprehended by the remarks given in the code.

Code

```
#working
import RPi.GPIO as IO   # calling for header file which helps in using GPIOs of PI
import time        # we are calling for time to provide delays in program
IO.setwarnings(False)   # do not show any warnings
IO.setmode (IO.BCM)     #programming the GPIO by
```

BCM pin numbers (like PIN29 as GPIO5)

```
IO.setup(21,IO.OUT)    # initialize GPIO21 as an output
IO.setup(20,IO.OUT)
IO.setup(16,IO.OUT)
IO.setup(12,IO.OUT)

IO.setup(27,IO.IN)    # initialize GPIO27 as an input
IO.setup(4,IO.IN)
IO.setup(22,IO.IN)
IO.setup(17,IO.IN)

while 1:
   if (IO.input(27) == 0): #If GPIO 27 goes low toggle
LED on 21pin and print RIGHT
     IO.output(21,1)
     time.sleep(0.01)
     IO.output(21,0)
     print ("RIGHT")

  if(IO.input(4) == 1): #If GPIO 4 goes high toggle LED
on 20pin and print LEFT
     IO.output(20,1)
     time.sleep(0.01)
     IO.output(20,0)
     print ("LEFT")

   if (IO.input(22) == 0): #If GPIO 22 goes low toggle
LED on 16pin and print UP
     IO.output(16,1)
     time.sleep(0.01)
     IO.output(16,0)
```

```
    print ("UP")

   if (IO.input(17) == 1):  #If GPIO 17 goes high toggle
LED on 12pin and print DOWN
    IO.output(12,1)
    time.sleep(0.01)
    IO.output(12,0)
    print ("DOWN")
```

◆ ◆ ◆

7. CONTROLLING RASPBERRY PI GPIO UTILIZING ANDROID APP OVER BLUETOOTH

Raspberry Pi is exceptionally well known for IoT ventures in light of its consistent capacity of remote correspondence over web. Raspberry Pi 3 has inbuilt Wi-Fi as well as Bluetooth, and Bluetooth is an extremely mainstream remote correspondence Protocol. We are gonna to Control Raspberry Pi GPIO Pin through an Android application utilizing Bluetooth.

Here we are utilizing Raspberry 2 Pi Model B which don't have inbuilt Bluetooth, so we are utilizing a straightforward USB Bluetooth dongle. Aside from that we just need a resistor (220R) and a LED to show the GPIO controlling. Here we are utilizing RFCOMM Bluetooth convention for remote correspondence.

Programming for Bluetooth in Python pursues the attachment programming model and correspondences between the Bluetooth gadgets is done through RFCOMM attachment. RFCOMM (Radio Frequency Communication) is a Bluetooth Protocol which gave copied RS-232 sequential ports and furthermore called as Serial Port Emulation. Bluetooth sequential port profile depends on this convention. RFCOMM is extremely well known in Bluetooth applications as a result of its wide help and publically accessible API. It is bound to L2CAP convention.

We have additionally utilized Bluetooth module HC-06 in our past undertaking: Voice controlled LEDs utilizing Raspberry Pi. Likewise check our past Raspberry Pi Projects alongside some great IoT Projects.

Installing Required Packages for Bluetooth Communication:

Prior to begin, we have to introduce a few virtual products for setting up Bluetooth correspondence in Raspberry Pi. You ought to have a Raspbian Jessie introduced memory card prepared with Raspberry Pi. Check this article to introduce the Raspbian OS and beginning with Raspberry Pi. So now we first need to refresh the Raspbian utilizing underneath directions:

```
sudo apt-get update
```

```
sudo apt-get upgrade
```

At that point we have to introduce not many Bluetooth related bundles:

```
sudo apt-get install bluetooth blueman bluez
```

At that point reboot the Raspberry Pi:

```
sudo reboot
```

BlueZ is an open source task and authority Linux Bluetooth convention stack. It underpins all the center Bluetooth conventions and now become piece of authentic Linux Kernel.

Blueman gives the Desktop interface to oversee and control the Bluetooth gadgets.

At last we need python Library for Bluetooth correspondence with the goal that we can send and get information through RFCOMM utilizing Python language:

```
sudo apt-get install python-bluetooth
```

Additionally introduce the GPIO bolster libraries for

Raspberry Pi:

```
sudo apt-get install python-rpi.gpio
```

Presently we are finished with introducing required bundles for Bluetooth correspondence in Raspberry Pi.

Pairing Devices with Raspberry Pi over Bluetooth:

Blending Bluetooth Devices, similar to cell phone, with Raspberry Pi is exceptionally simple. Here we have matched our Android Smart telephone with Raspberry Pi. We have recently introduced BlueZ in Pi, which gives a direction line utility called "bluetoothctl" to deal with our Bluetooth gadgets. Yet, before that, associate your USB Bluetooth dongle with Raspberry Pi and watch that whether it is recognized or not, by utilizing underneath direction:

```
lsusb
```

Presently open the bluetoothctl utility by underneath order:

```
sudo bluetoothctl
```

You can check every one of the directions of bluetoothctl utility by composing 'help'. Until further notice we have to enter underneath directions in given request:

```
[bluetooth]# power on

[bluetooth]# agent on

[bluetooth]# discoverable on

[bluetooth]# pairable on

[bluetooth]# scan on
```

After the keep going direction "examine on", you will see your Bluetooth gadget (Mobile telephone) in the rundown. Ensure that your versatile has Bluetooth turned on and obvious by close by gadgets. At that point duplicate the MAC address of you gadget and pair it by utilizing given order:

> pair <address of your phone>

At that point you will be incited for Passcode or Pin in your Terminal support at that point type password there and press enter. At that point type the equivalent password in your cell phone when provoked and you are presently effectively matched with Raspberry Pi.

As told before, you can likewise utilize Desktop interface to match the Mobile telephone. In the wake of introducing Blueman, you will see a Bluetooth symbol in right half of your Raspberry Pi work area as demonstrated as follows, utilizing which you can without much of a stretch do the blending.

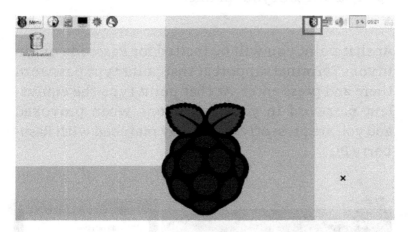

Circuit Diagram:

Circuit outline is straightforward, we simply associated a LED to PIN 40 (GPIO 21) of Raspberry Pi with a resistor of 220 Ohm:

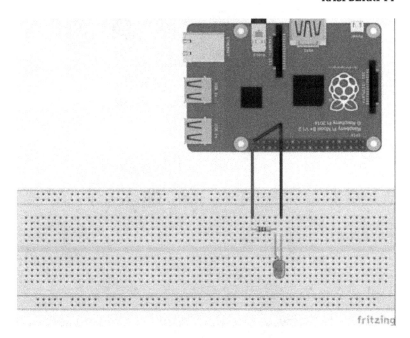

fritzing

Controlling LED with Android App BlueTerm:

Presently in the wake of paring the Mobile Phone, we have to introduce an Android App for speaking with Raspberry Pi utilizing a Bluetooth Serial Adapter. As told before RFCOMM/SPP convention imitates sequential correspondence over Bluetooth, so we introduced here BlueTerm App which bolsters this convention.

Terminal emulator to connect to any serial
device with bluetooth serial adapter.

You can likewise utilize some other Bluetooth
Terminal App which underpins correspondence by
means of RFCOMM attachment.

Presently subsequent to downloading and introducing the BlueTerm App, run the underneath given Python Program from the terminal and associate the matched raspberrypi gadget from the BlueTerm App simultaneously.

After effective association you will see connected:raspberrypi at the upper right corner of the App as demonstrated as follows:

Presently you can simply enter '1' or '0' from the Blue-Term application to make the GPIO pin HIGH as well as LOW individually, which in kills switch ON and the LED associated with this pin. Press 'q' to leave the program. You can utilize Google Voice Typing Keyboard to control the GPIO utilizing your Voice.

So this is the manner by which you can remotely control the GPIO Pin utilizing an Android App over Bluetooth. Likewise check How to utilize Bluetooth with Arduino.

Programming Explanation:

Python Program for Controlling Raspberry Pi GPIO with Android App is straightforward and plain as day. Just we have to adapt tad about the code identified with Bluetooth RFCOMM correspondence. First we have to import the Bluetooth attachment library which empowers us to control Bluetooth with Python language; we have introduced the library for the equivalent in the past segment.

```
import Bluetooth
```

The following is the code answerable for Bluetooth correspondence:

```
server_socket=bluetooth.Bluetooth-
Socket( bluetooth.RFCOMM )

port = 1

server_socket.bind(("",port))

server_socket.listen(1)
```

```
client_socket,address = server_socket.accept()

print "Accepted connection from ",address

while 1:

data = client_socket.recv(1024)
```

Here we can comprehend them line by line:

server_socket=bluetooth.Bluetooth-Socket(bluetooth.RFCOMM): Creating attachment for Bluetooth RFCOMM correspondence.

server_socket.bind(("", port):- Server ties the content on have " to port.

server_socket.listen(1): Server tunes in to acknowledge each association in turn.

client_socket, address = server_socket.accept(): Server acknowledges customer's association ask for and allot the macintosh address to the variable location, client_socket is the customer's attachment

information = client_socket.recv(1024): Receive information through the customer attachment client_socket and allocate it to the variable information. Greatest 1024 characters can be gotten at once.

At long last after all the programming, close the customer and server association utilizing underneath code:

```
client_socket.close()

server_socket.close()
```

The various code is simple and clear as crystal. Check the full code beneath. Attempt to change this task and you can utilize it to control numerous different things remotely, such as utilizing Relays you can control the home machines or can likewise control a Robot vehicle through android telephone.

Code

```
import bluetooth
import RPi.GPIO as GPIO       #calling for header file which helps in using GPIOs of PI
LED=21


GPIO.setmode(GPIO.BCM)    #programming the GPIO by BCM pin numbers. (like PIN40 as GPIO21)
GPIO.setwarnings(False)
GPIO.setup(LED,GPIO.OUT) #initialize GPIO21 (LED) as an output Pin
GPIO.output(LED,0)
```

```python
server_socket=bluetooth.Bluetooth-
Socket(bluetooth.RFCOMM)


port = 1
server_socket.bind(("",port))
server_socket.listen(1)


client_socket,address = server_socket.accept()
print "Accepted connection from ",address
while 1:

 data = client_socket.recv(1024)
 print "Received: %s" % data
 if (data == "0"):   #if '0' is sent from the Android App,
turn OFF the LED
 print ("GPIO 21 LOW, LED OFF")
 GPIO.output(LED,0)
 if (data == "1"):   #if '1' is sent from the Android App,
turn OFF the LED
 print ("GPIO 21 HIGH, LED ON")
 GPIO.output(LED,1)
 if (data == "q"):
 print ("Quit")
 break

client_socket.close()
server_socket.close()
```

8. RASPBERRY PI ALARM CLOCK UTILIZING RTC MODULE DS1307

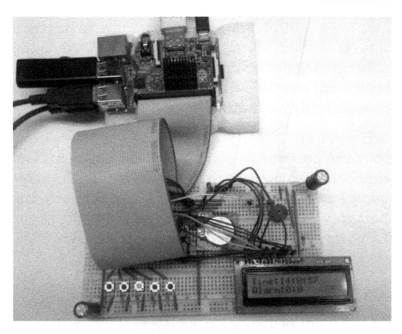

We are gonna to Interface Real Time Clock Module DS1307 with Raspberry PI to make an Alarm Clock. In spite of the fact that Raspberry Pi has an inner clock, however without web association this interior clock resets after each reboot. So to get precise TIME without web association, we have to interface a RTC Module DS1307 to Raspberry Pi. RTC module has button battery for reinforcement so the TIME won't reset. We have likewise constructed Alarm Clock utilizing Arduino and utilizing ATmega32 AVR Micro-controller, check them as well.

In this Raspberry Pi Digital Clock, a 16*2 Character Liquid Crystal Display is to show Real Time, Alarm time as well as status of the caution (ON/OFF). When the program begins running in Pi, we can disengage the screen and can set the caution with the assistance of this LCD and five catches.

Every one of 17 GPIO pins can convey or draw a limit of 15mA current. So don't play with GPIO pins and check the associations twice before fueling the Raspberry Pi. Get familiar with GPIO Pins and interfacing button with Raspberry Pi here. Likewise check our Raspberry Pi Tutorial Series alongside some great IoT Projects.

Components Required:

Here we are utilizing Raspberry Pi 2 Model B with Raspbian Jessie OS. All the fundamental Hardware and Software necessities are recently talked about, you can find it in the Raspberry Pi Introduction and Raspberry PI LED Blinking for beginning, other than that we need:

- Raspberry Pi with pre-installed OS
- RTC Module DS1307 with Battery
- Power supply
- 1K? resistor (six pieces)
- 5 buttons
- 1000uF capacitor (2 pieces)
- 16*2 character LCD
- 2N2222 transistor
- Buzzer

Setup Raspberry Pi for Alarm clock:

Before going any further, we have to design Raspberry Pi a smidgen and introduce the library document for RTC Module, pursue underneath steps:

Stage 1: First go to Raspberry Pi arrangement menu and empower I2C choice as demonstrated as follows:

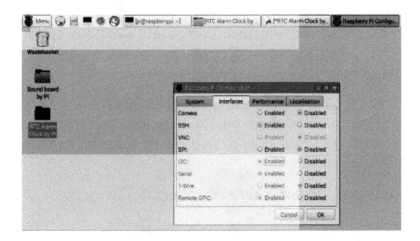

Stage 2: Create another envelope on Raspberry Pi work area screen and name it as "Morning timer"

Stage 3: Download the Header File for RTC module from beneath connect:

https://codeload.github.com/switchdoclabs/RTC_S-DL_DS1307/zip/ace

Stage 4: Unzip the downloaded compress document into the envelope (Alarm Clock) made on DESKTOP, as told in past advance.

Stage 5: Open the terminal window in Raspberry Pi and enter beneath order, at that point press enter:

```
sudo apt-get install i2c-tools
```

This order introduces I2C apparatuses required for interfacing RTC module. At that point reboot the Raspberry pi by giving 'sudo reboot' order.

Stage 6: Now we have to check the I2C address of RTC module. Before checking the location, first interface the RTC module as appeared in the Circuit Diagram beneath.

At that point enter beneath in terminal window.

```
sudo i2cdetect -y 0

OR

sudo i2cdetect -y 1
```

Stage 7: If both of above directions works, you will see something like this:

Stage 8: You will see I2C address 0x68 if RTC module is associated appropriately, record the worth.

With this all the essential changes are finished with Raspberry Pi design.

Circuit Diagram and Connections:

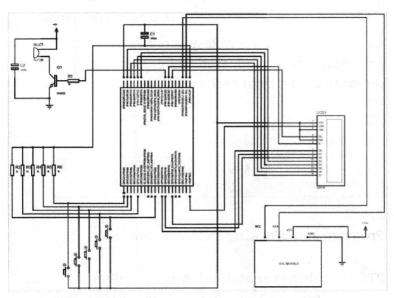

Associations between Raspberry Pi and LCD are appeared in underneath table:

LCD connection	PI connection
GND	GND
VCC	+5V
VEE	GND
RS	GPIO17
R/W	GND
EN	GPIO27
D0	GPIO24
D1	GPIO23
D2	GPIO18
D3	GPIO26
D4	GPIO5
D5	GPIO6
D6	GPIO13
D7	GPIO19

Associations between Raspberry Pi and five catches are additionally appeared in beneath table with the separate capacity of each catch:

Button	PI connection	Function
1	GPIO21	ALARM HOUR INCREMENT
2	GPIO20	ALARM HOUR DECREMENT
3	GPIO16	ALARM MINUTE INCREMENT
4	GPIO12	ALARM MINUTE DECREMENT
5	GPIO25	ALARM ON/OFF

Program and Working Explanation:

RTC Module has a catch cell for control reinforcement as examined, so the time will be cutting-edge until the reinforcement runs out and we will have exact time in RTC.

Presently we will compose a Python Program to get the precise time from RTC Module DS1307. This time will be appeared on the 16x2 LCD. After that we will have morning timer highlight written in program. The caution time will likewise be shown on the second line of LCD, trailed by ON and OFF status. Caution time can be balanced by 5 catches associated with Raspberry Pi as referenced in the table given above and it is extremely simple to set the Alarm. There are 2 catches for increase and decrement Alarm Hour time, 2 catches for increase and decrement Alarm Minute time and 1 catch for ON and OFF the alert.

Python program continues contrasting the Alarm Time and RTC Time persistently and once the Alarm time matches with the RTC time, PI triggers the Buzzer, which is associated with GPIO pin 22 of Raspberry Pi through the NPN transistor 2N2222. So once the alert time came to, ringer makes the sound.

Complete Program is given beneath, and very much clarified through the remarks.

Code

```
import RPi.GPIO as IO  #calling for header file which
helps in using GPIO's of PI
import time       #we are calling for time to provide
delays in program
import datetime    #we are calling for DATE
import SDL_DS1307   #calling for special functions
```

which helps us interface RTC module
```
h=0          #integers for storing values
m=0
alarm=0
string_of_characters = 0
```

```
ds1307 = SDL_DS1307.SDL_DS1307(1, 0x68) #enter-
```
ing I2c address, which we recorded previously
```
ds1307.write_now()
```

```
IO.setwarnings(False) #do not show any warnings
IO.setmode (IO.BCM)    #programming the GPIO by
```
BCM pin numbers. (like PIN29 as 'GPIO5')

```
#initialize  GPIO17,27,24,23,18,26,5,6,13,19  as  an
output
IO.setup(17,IO.OUT)
IO.setup(27,IO.OUT)
IO.setup(24,IO.OUT)
IO.setup(23,IO.OUT)
IO.setup(18,IO.OUT)
IO.setup(26,IO.OUT)
IO.setup(5,IO.OUT)
IO.setup(6,IO.OUT)
IO.setup(13,IO.OUT)
IO.setup(19,IO.OUT)
```

```
IO.setup(21,IO.IN) #initialize GPIO21 as an input.
IO.setup(20,IO.IN) #initialize GPIO20 as an input.
IO.setup(16,IO.IN)
IO.setup(12,IO.IN)
IO.setup(25,IO.IN)
```

```
IO.setup(22,IO.OUT) #initialize GPIO22 as an output.

def send_a_command (command): #steps for sending
a command to 16*2LCD
  pin=command
  PORT(pin);
  IO.output(17,0)
  IO.output(27,1)
  time.sleep(0.001)
  IO.output(27,0)
  pin=0
  PORT(pin);

def send_a_character (character):#steps for sending a
character to 16*2 LCD
  pin=character
  PORT(pin);
  IO.output(17,1)
  IO.output(27,1)
  time.sleep(0.001)
  IO.output(27,0)
  pin=0
  PORT(pin);

def PORT(pin):          #assigning level for PI GPIO for
sending data to LCD through D0-D7
  if(pin&0x01 == 0x01):
    IO.output(24,1)
  else:
    IO.output(24,0)
  if(pin&0x02 == 0x02):
    IO.output(23,1)
```

```python
else:
  IO.output(23,0)
if(pin&0x04 == 0x04):
  IO.output(18,1)
else:
  IO.output(18,0)
if(pin&0x08 == 0x08):
  IO.output(26,1)
else:
  IO.output(26,0)
if(pin&0x10 == 0x10):
  IO.output(5,1)
else:
  IO.output(5,0)
if(pin&0x20 == 0x20):
  IO.output(6,1)
else:
  IO.output(6,0)
if(pin&0x40 == 0x40):
  IO.output(13,1)
else:
  IO.output(13,0)
if(pin&0x80 == 0x80):
  IO.output(19,1)
else:
  IO.output(19,0)

def send_a_string(string_of_characters):   #steps for
sending string of characters to LCD
    string_of_characters = string_of_characters.l-
just(16,"")
```

```python
for i in range(16):
    send_a_character(ord(string_of_characters[i]))
#send characters one by one until all the strings char-
acters are sent through data port

while 1:
    send_a_command(0x38); #use two lines of LCD
    send_a_command(0x0E); #screen and cursor ON
    send_a_command(0x01); #clear screen
    time.sleep(0.1)    #sleep for 100msec
    while 1:
        if(IO.input(21) == 0):
            if(h<23):  #if button1 is pressed and hour count
is less than 23 increment 'h' by one
                h=h+1

        if(IO.input(20) == 0):
            if(h>0):  #if button2 is pressed and hour count is
more than 0 decrease 'h' by one
                h=h-1

        if(IO.input(16) == 0):
            if(m<59):   #if button3 is pressed and minute
count is less than 59 increment 'm' by one
                m=m+1

        if(IO.input(12) == 0):
            if(m>0):  #if button4 is pressed and minute count
is more than 0 decrease 'm' by one
                m=m-1

        if(IO.input(25) == 0): #if button5 is pressed toggle
Alarm ON and OFF
```

```python
    if(alarm==0):
      alarm=1
    else:
      alarm=0
    time.sleep(0.1)

  if(alarm==1):
    send_a_command(0x80 + 0x40 + 12);
    send_a_string("ON"); #if alarm is set, then display
"ON" at the 12th position of second line of LCD

    if((h==ds1307._read_hours())):
      if((m==ds1307._read_minutes())):
              IO.output(22,1)  #if alarm is set, and
hour-minute settings match the RTC time, trigger the
buzzer

  if(alarm==0):
    send_a_command(0x80 + 0x40 + 12);
    send_a_string("OFF"); #if alarm is OFF, then dis-
play "OFF" at the 12th position of second line of LCD
    IO.output(22,0)    #turn off the buzzer

  send_a_command(0x80 + 0); #move courser to 0
position
              send_a_string  ("Time:%s:%s:%s"
% (ds1307._read_hours(),ds1307._read_minutes(),d-
s1307._read_seconds()));
  #display RTC hours, minutes, seconds
  send_a_command(0x80 + 0x40 + 0); #move cour-
ser to second line
    send_a_string ("Alarm:%s:%s" % (h,m)); #show
alarm time
```

time.sleep(0.1) #wait for 100msec

9. USE PYGAME LIBRARY TO PLAY GAME SOUNDS WITH RASPBERRY PI

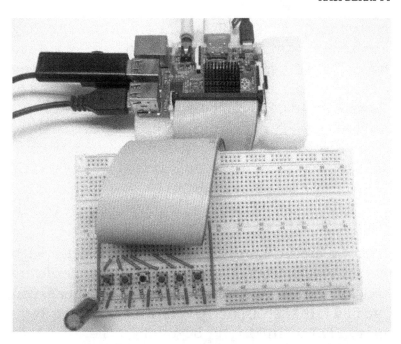

We are gonna to utilize Raspberry Pi as well as the PYGAME capacities to make a sound board. In straightforward terms, we will associate barely any catches to the Raspberry Pi GPIO pins and when these catches are squeezed Raspberry Pi plays sound records put away in its memory. These sound records can be played individually or they would all be able to be played together. As it were you can squeeze one or different fastens simultaneously, Raspberry Pi will play one or various sound records appropriately simultaneously. Additionally check our Raspberry Pi Tutorial Series alongside some great IoT Projects.

We have 26 GPIO sticks in Raspberry Pi which can be

customized, out of which some are utilized to play out some uncommon capacities and afterward we have 17 GPIO remaining. Each GPIO pin can convey or draw a limit of 15mA. What's more, the entirety of flows from all GPIO can't surpass 50mA. So we can attract a limit of 3mA normal from every one of these GPIO pins. We will utilize resistors to restrict the present stream. Study GPIO Pins as well as interfacing button with Raspberry Pi here.

Components Required:

Here we are utilizing Raspberry Pi 2 Model B with Raspbian Jessie OS. All the fundamental Hardware and Software necessities are recently examined, you can find it in the Raspberry Pi Introduction and Raspberry PI LED Blinking for beginning, other than that we need:

- Raspberry Pi with pre-installed OS
- Speaker
- Power supply
- Push Buttons (six pieces)
- 1K? resistor (six pieces)
- 1000uF capacitor

Working Explanation:

Here we are Playing Sound utilizing Buttons with Raspberry Pi. We have utilized 6 push catches to play 6 sound documents. We can include more fastens and sound records to stretch out this board to make progressively wonderful example by squeezing these catches. Before clarifying any further, total the means beneath.

1. Most importantly download the 6 Audio records from the connection given underneath or you can utilize your sound documents, however then you have to change the document names in Code.

Download Audio documents from here

2. Make another organizer on Raspberry Pi work area screen and name it as "PI SOUND BOARD".

3. Unfasten the downloaded sound documents into the organizer which we have made on DESKTOP in past advance.

4. Open the terminal window in Raspberry Pi and enter beneath order:

```
sudo amixer cset numid=3 1  <press enter>
```

This direction advises PI to give sound yield through 3.5mm sound jack ready.

In case you need sound yield from HDMI Port, in that moment you can use beneath direction:

```
$ sudo amixer cset numid=3 2 <press enter>
```

5. Interface speakers to the 3.5mm sound yield jack on the Raspberry Pi board.

6. Make a PYTHON document (*.py augmentation) and spare it in a similar envelope. Check this instructional exercise for making and running the Python Program in Raspberry Pi.

7. Pygame blender will be introduced as a matter of course in the OS. In the event that the program, after execution, doesn't review PYMIXER, at that point update the OS of Raspberry Pi by entering underneath direction in the terminal window. Ensure that Pi is associated with web.

```
sudo apt-get update <press enter>
```

Hang tight for few moments for the OS to refresh.

Presently interface each part according to the circuit outline given underneath, Copy the PYHTON program into the PYHTON document made on the work area lastly hit race to play the sound records through the catches. Python Program is given toward the end.

Circuit Diagram:

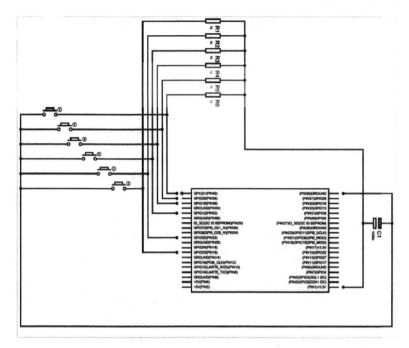

Programming Explanation:

Here we have made Python Program to play the Audio Files as per button press. Here we have to comprehend hardly any directions, which we have utilized in the program.

```
import RPi.GPIO as IO
```

We are gonna to import GPIO document from library, above order empowers us to program GPIO pins of PI. We are likewise renaming "GPIO" to "IO", so in the program at whatever point we need to allude to GPIO pins we will utilize the word 'IO'.

```
IO.setwarnings(False)
```

Once in a while, when the GPIO pins which we are attempting to utilize may be doing some different capacities. At that point you will recipient admonitions at whatever point you execute a program. This order discloses to Raspberry Pi to disregard the admonitions and continue with the program.

```
IO.setmode (IO.BCM)
```

Here we will allude I/o pins of PI by their capacity name. So we are modifying the GPIO by BCM pin numbers, which empowers us to call PINs with their GPIO pin no. Like we can call PIN39 as GPIO19 in the program.

```
import pygame.mixer
```

We are calling pygame blender to play the sound documents.

```
audio1 = pygame.mixer.Sound("buzzer.wav")
```

We are calling for 'buzzer.wav' sound document put away in work area envelope. In the event that you need to play some other record, simply change the sound document name in the capacity given previously. You can name any records present in the work area envelope.

```
channel1 = pygame.mixer.Channel(1)
```

Here we are setting up a channel for each catch so we can play all sound documents at the same time.

```
if(IO.input(21) == 0):

    channel1.play(audio1)
```

In case, the condition in if proclamation is valid, the announcement underneath it will be executed once. So on the off chance that the GPIO pin 21 goes low or grounded, at that point it will play the sound record relegated to audio1 variable. According to Circuit Diagram, we can see that GPIO pin 21 goes low when we press first catch. So we can play any sound record by squeezing the comparing button.

while 1: is utilized as everlastingly circle, with this order the announcements inside this circle will be executed ceaselessly.

You can make changes to the python program to make the most fulfilling Sound Board with Raspberry Pi. You can even add more fastens to make things all the more fascinating and play more sound records.
Code

```
#working
import pygame.mixer #calling for pygame mixer to play audio files
import time     #calling for time to provide delays in program
import RPi.GPIO as IO  #calling for header file which helps in using GPIO's of PI

IO.setwarnings(False) #do not show any warnings
IO.setmode(IO.BCM)    #programming the GPIO by BCM pin numbers. (like PIN29 as'GPIO5')

IO.setup(21, IO.IN) #initialize GPIO21 as an input
IO.setup(20, IO.IN) #initialize GPIO20 as an input
IO.setup(16, IO.IN) #initialize GPIO16 as an input
IO.setup(12, IO.IN) #initialize GPIO12 as an input
IO.setup(25, IO.IN) #initialize GPIO25 as an input
IO.setup(23, IO.IN) #initialize GPIO23 as an input

pygame.mixer.init(48000, -16, 1, 1024) #initializing audio mixer

audio1 = pygame.mixer.Sound("buzzer.wav")   #calling for audio file
audio2 = pygame.mixer.Sound("cartoon002.wav") #calling for audio file
audio3 = pygame.mixer.Sound("baby_x.wav")   #call-
```

```
ing for audio file
audio4    =    pygame.mixer.Sound("ahem_x.wav")
#calling for audio file
audio5 = pygame.mixer.Sound("clap.wav")
audio6 = pygame.mixer.Sound("baseball_hit.wav")

channel1 = pygame.mixer.Channel(1)   #using chan-
nel one for first button
channel2 = pygame.mixer.Channel(2)   #using chan-
nel two for second button
channel3 = pygame.mixer.Channel(3)   #using chan-
nel three for second button
channel4 = pygame.mixer.Channel(4)   #using chan-
nel four for second button
channel5 = pygame.mixer.Channel(5)   #using chan-
nel five for second button
channel6 = pygame.mixer.Channel(6)   #using chan-
nel six for second button

while 1: #execute loop forever
  if(IO.input(21) == 0):
        channel1.play(audio1)       #if button one is
pressed(grounded) play audio file one

  if(IO.input(20) == 0):
        channel2.play(audio2)       #if button two is
pressed(grounded) play second audio file

  if(IO.input(16) == 0):
        channel3.play(audio3)       #if button three is
pressed(grounded) play third audio file

  if(IO.input(12) == 0):
```

```
    channel4.play(audio4)

if(IO.input(25) == 0):
    channel5.play(audio5)

if(IO.input(23) == 0):
    channel6.play(audio6)

time.sleep(.01) #sleep for 100ms
```

10. 3X3X3 LIGHT EMITTING DIODE CUBE WITH RASPBERRY PI AND PYTHON PROGRAM

We have made a progression of Raspberry Pi Tutorials, in which we have secured Interfacing of Raspberry Pi with all the fundamental parts like LED, LCD, button, DC engine, Servo Motor, Stepper Motor, ADC, move Register, and so forth. We have likewise distributed some basic Raspberry Pi ventures for amateurs, alongside some great IoT ventures. We are gonna to make a 3x3x3 Light Emitting Diode CUBE as well as manage it by Raspberry Pi to get various examples utilizing the Python Programming. We have beforehand assemble the equivalent 3x3x3 Light Emitting Diode Cube with Arduino Uno.

An ordinary 3*3*3 LED shape associated with Raspberry Pi is appeared in the picture above. This LED CUBE is made of 27 Light Emitting Diodes, these 27 LEDs are orchestrated in lines and segments to frame a 3D square. Subsequently the name is LED CUBE.

There are numerous sorts of blocks that can be planned. The most straightforward one of them is 3*3*3 LED solid shape. For 4*4*4 LED CUBE, the work is practically triple occasions since we have to do work for 64 LED. With each higher number the work nearly pairs or triples. Be that as it may, each 3D shape pretty much chips away at a similar way. For an apprentice, 3*3*3 LED 3D square is the least complex LED CUBE and furthermore there are a few favorable circumstances of 3x3x3 LED Cube over other higher Cubes like,

- For this 3D shape you need not stress over power utilization or dispersal.

- Power supply request is less.

- We needn't bother with any exchanging hardware for this 3D square.

- We need lesser rationale terminals so we needn't bother with move registers or anything like that.

- Most appropriate for +3.3v rationale worked hardware like Raspberry Pi.

Components Required:

Here we are utilizing Raspberry Pi 2 Model B with Raspbian Jessie OS. All the essential Hardware and Software necessities are recently examined, you can find it in the Raspberry Pi Introduction and Raspberry PI LED Blinking for beginning, other than that we need:

- Raspberry Pi 2 B (any model)
- 27 Light Emitting Diodes
- 220? resisters (three pieces)
- Soldering tools for building Light Emitting Diode Cube

Building 3x3x3 LED Cube:

We have recently talked about the structure of 3*3*3 LED solid shape in detail in this article: 3x3x3 LED Cube with Arduino. You should check this one for figuring out how to patch LEDs for framing LED Cube. Here we are referencing 9 Common positive terminals (sections) and 3 normal negative terminals (Negative Rows or layers) in LED Cube. Every section speaks to a positive terminal and each layer speaks to a negative terminal.

We can view nine Common +ve Terminals from the Top View as numbered in the underneath images, we have numbered them according to the GPIO pin no of

Raspberry Pi, on which these positive terminals are associated.

Nine Common +ve Terminals: 4, 17, 27, 24, 23, 18, 25, 12, 16

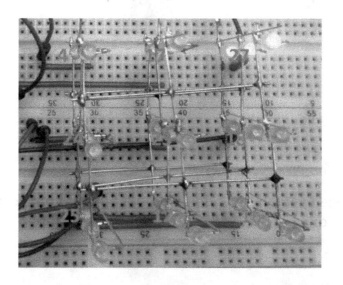

Also, the three Common -ve Terminals can be viewed from Front View as numbered in the beneath Picture:

Top Layer basic negative pin: 13

Center Layer basic negative pin: 6

Base Layer basic negative pin: 5

Once everything is done you will have a block like this one.

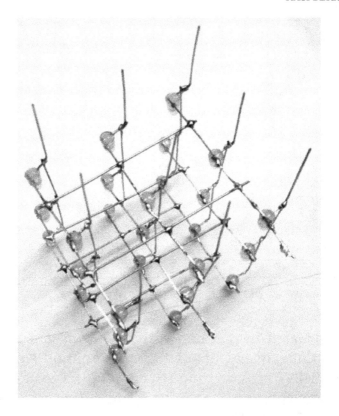

Circuit Diagram and Explanation:

Associations between Raspberry Pi and LED Cube are appeared in beneath Circuit Diagram:

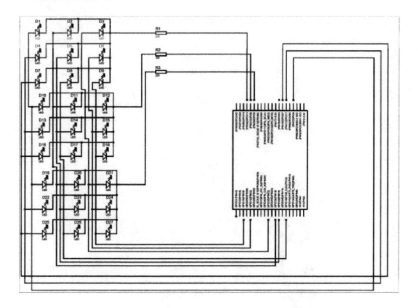

As appeared in picture, we have a sum of 12 pins from Cube, over which NINE are Common Positive and THREE are Common Negative Pins. Recall every segment speaks to a positive terminal and each layer speaks to a negative terminal.

Presently we will associate these 12 pins to Raspberry Pi precisely as given in the circuit chart. When we have associated the terminals it's an ideal opportunity to compose the PYTHON program.

You can check the Python program underneath to produce the example.

State, we need to turn on LED on the center layer as showed in beneath picture (red surrounded), at that point we have to control the GPIO18 pin and ground the GPIO6 pin. This goes for each LED in the 3D shape.

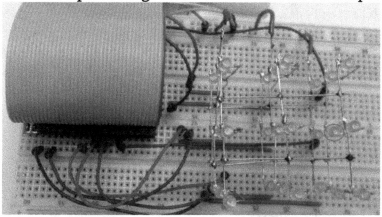

We have composed couple of circle programs in PY-THON to make straightforward flashes. Program is very much clarified through the remarks. In the event that you need more examples you would simple be able to add more examples in to the program.

Code

```
#working
import RPi.GPIO as IO  #calling for header file which helps in using GPIO's of PI
import time      #calling for time to provide delays in program
IO.setwarnings(False) #do not show any warnings
x=1
y=1
z=0
```

```
IO.setmode (IO.BCM)
IO.setup(4,IO.OUT)  #initialize GPIO4 as an output
IO.setup(17,IO.OUT)  #initialize GPIO17 as an output
IO.setup(27,IO.OUT)  #initialize GPIO27 as an output
IO.setup(24,IO.OUT)
IO.setup(23,IO.OUT)
IO.setup(18,IO.OUT)
IO.setup(25,IO.OUT)
IO.setup(12,IO.OUT)
IO.setup(16,IO.OUT)
IO.setup(5,IO.OUT)
IO.setup(6,IO.OUT)
IO.setup(13,IO.OUT)

columns = [4,17,27,24,23,18,25,12,16] #GPIO pins of
columns in order
rows =[5,6,13] #GPIO pins of rows in order
random = [4,24,25,17,23,12,27,18,16]  #GPIO pins of
columns in random

for z in range (3):
  IO.output(rows[z],1)   #pulling up the rows
for z in range (9):
    IO.output(columns[z],0)   #pulling down the col-
umns

while 1:
  for y in range (3):   #execute the loop 3 times incre-
menting y value from zero to three
    IO.output(rows[y],0) #pull down the rows pointed
by 'y'
    for x in range (9):  #execute the loop 9 times incre-
```

menting x value from zero to eight

```
        IO.output(columns[x],1) #pull up the columns
pointed by 'x'
    time.sleep(0.1)      #sleep for 100ms
    IO.output(columns[x],0) #pull down the columns
after 100ms
        IO.output(rows[y],1)        #pull up the row after
100ms

  for y in range (3):
    IO.output(rows[2-y],0)
    for x in range (9):
      IO.output(columns[8-x],1)
      time.sleep(0.1)
      IO.output(columns[8-x],0)
    IO.output(rows[2-y],1)

  for y in range (3):
    IO.output(rows[y],0)


  for x in range (9):
    IO.output(columns[x],1)
    time.sleep(0.1)
    IO.output(columns[x],0)

  for y in range (3):
    IO.output(rows[y],1)

  for y in range (3):
    IO.output(rows[2-y],0)

  for x in range (9):
    IO.output(columns[8-x],1)
```

```
    time.sleep(0.1)
    IO.output(columns[8-x],0)
  for y in range (3):
    IO.output(rows[2-y],1)

  for y in range (3):
    IO.output(rows[y],0)
    for x in range (9):
      IO.output(random[x],1)
      time.sleep(0.1)
      IO.output(random[x],0)
    IO.output(rows[y],1)

  for y in range (3):
    IO.output(rows[2-y],0)
    for x in range (9):
      IO.output(random[8-x],1)
      time.sleep(0.1)
      IO.output(random[8-x],0)
    IO.output(rows[2-y],1)
```

Thank You !!!

Thank
You!!!